Ivy Global

ISEE
LOWER LEVEL
TESTS
1ST EDITION

IVY GLOBAL, NEW YORK

This publication was written and edited by the team at Ivy Global.

Editors: Corwin Henville and Laurel Perkins
Layout Editor: Sacha Azor
Contributors: Sarah Atkins, Ali Candib, Tamara Jordan, Nathan Létourneau, Sarah Pike, and Julia Romanski
Producers: Lloyd Min and Junho Suh

About Ivy Global

Ivy Global is a pioneering education company that provides a wide range of educational services.

E-mail: info@ivyglobal.com
Website: http://www.ivyglobal.com

CONTENTS

INTRODUCTION
CHAPTER 1

HOW TO USE THIS BOOK

Welcome, students and parents! This book is intended for students practicing for the Lower Level Independent School Entrance Exam (ISEE). For students applying to many top private and independent schools in North America, the ISEE is a crucial and sometimes daunting step in the admissions process. By exposing you to the format of the ISEE, Ivy Global will help you build your confidence and maximize your score on this important exam.

This book is right for you if:

- you are applying to a private or independent school that requires the ISEE for admission
- you will be in Grades 4-5 when you take the ISEE
- you would like to practice for the ISEE exam using full-length practice tests under simulated testing conditions
- you are a parent, family member, or tutor looking for new ways to help your Lower Level ISEE student

We know that no two students are exactly alike—each student brings a unique combination of personal strengths and weaknesses to his or her test preparation. For this reason, we've tailored our preparation materials to help students with a specific subject area or goal.

Ivy Global's *ISEE English* includes the best strategies for the ISEE Verbal Reasoning and Reading Comprehension sections, plus a step-by-step approach to the Essay section and a thorough vocabulary and writing skills review.

Ivy Global's *ISEE Math* includes the best strategies for the ISEE Quantitative Reasoning and Mathematics Achievement sections, plus thorough review and practice for all of the math concepts tested at each level.

Ivy Global's products are available for purchase at ivyglobal.com/products or amazon.com.

This book includes:

- an up-to-date introduction to the ISEE's administration, format, and scoring practices
- instructions for taking a full-length practice test for the ISEE under simulated testing conditions
- 2 full-length practice tests for the ISEE Lower Level
- detailed scoring instructions for the exam

To make the best use of this book, take time to assess your strengths and weaknesses after you have worked through an exam. Then, spend some time reviewing the concepts you found challenging before you test yourself again.

To get started, continue reading for an overview of the ISEE. Good luck in this exciting new step for your education!

ABOUT THE ISEE

The **ISEE (Independent School Entrance Exam)** is a standardized test administered to students in grades 1-11 to help determine placement into certain private and independent schools. Many secondary schools worldwide use the ISEE as an integral part of their admissions process. The ISEE is owned and published by the Educational Records Bureau.

You will register for one of four ISEE tests, depending on your grade level:

- The **Primary Level** exam is for students currently in grades 1-3.
- The **Lower Level** exam is for students currently in grades 4-5.
- The **Middle Level** exam is for students currently in grades 6-7.
- The **Upper Level** exam is for students currently in grades 8-11.

The Primary Level exam is administered only with the use of a computer, and includes auditory content. All other levels may be taken on a computer or in a paper-and-pencil format. Among levels, the exams differ in difficulty, length, and the types of questions that may appear. The Lower Level exam is shorter than the Middle or Upper level exams.

WHEN IS THE TEST ADMINISTERED?

Administration dates for the ISEE vary between test locations. ISEE test sites and administration dates can be found online, at ERBlearn.org. In addition to taking the test at a school that administers large group tests, students applying to grades 5-12 can register to take the ISEE at a Prometric Testing Center, which administers computer-based exams.

HOW MANY TIMES CAN I TAKE THE TEST?

Students may only take the ISEE once per admission season. The version of the test doesn't matter: a student who has taken a paper-and-pencil test may not take another test on a computer, and a student who has taken a computer-based test may not take another test in a paper-and-pencil format.

HOW DO I REGISTER?

The easiest and fastest way to register is to complete the **online application**. Visit www.ERBlearn.org to register for an exam in your area. It is also possible to register over the phone by calling (800) 446-0320 or (919) 956-8524, or to register by mail. To register by mail, you must complete and submit the application form available only in the printed ISEE student guide. Visit www.ERBlearn.org to order a printed copy of the ISEE student guide.

WHAT IS THE FORMAT OF THE ISEE?

The Lower, Middle, and Upper Level ISEE exams consist of four scored sections (**Verbal Reasoning**, **Quantitative Reasoning**, **Reading Comprehension**, and **Mathematics Achievement**), plus an **Essay** that is used as a writing sample. The format of the test differs based on the level of the exam:

LOWER LEVEL			
Section	**Questions**	**Length**	**Topics Covered**
Verbal Reasoning	34	20 min	Synonyms, Sentence Completion
Quantitative Reasoning	38	35 min	Logical Reasoning, Pattern Recognition (Word Problems)
Reading Comprehension	25	25 min	Short Passages
Math Achievement	30	30 min	Arithmetic, Algebra, Geometry, Data Analysis
Essay	1	30 min	One age-appropriate essay prompt
Total testing time: 2 hours 20 minutes			

Ivy Global

MIDDLE AND UPPER LEVEL			
Section	Questions	Length	Topics Covered
Verbal Reasoning	40	20 min	Synonyms, Sentence Completion
Quantitative Reasoning	37	35 min	Logical Reasoning, Pattern Recognition (Word Problems and Quantitative Comparison)
Reading Comprehension	36	35 min	Short Passages
Math Achievement	47	40 min	Arithmetic, Algebra, Geometry, Data Analysis
Essay	1	30 min	One age-appropriate essay prompt
Total testing time: 2 hours 40 minutes			

Except for the Essay, all questions are **multiple-choice** (A) to (D). You are not normally allowed to use calculators, rulers, dictionaries, or other aids during the exam. However, students with documented learning disabilities or physical challenges may apply to take the test with extra time, aids, or other necessary accommodations that they receive in school. For more information about taking the ISEE with a documented disability, visit the ISEE Website at ERBlearn.org.

HOW IS THE ISEE SCORED?

All of the multiple-choice questions on the ISEE are equal in value, and your **raw score** for these sections is the total number of questions answered correctly. There is no penalty for incorrect answers.

Within each section, there are also 5-6 **experimental questions** that do not count towards your raw score for the section. The ISEE uses these questions to measure exam accuracy and to test material for upcoming exams. You won't be told which questions are the experimental questions, however, so you have to do your best on the entire section.

Your raw score for each section is then converted into a **scaled score** that represents how well you did in comparison to other students who have taken the same exam. Scaled scores range from about 760-950 for each section, with total scaled scores ranging from about 2280-2850.

The **Essay** is not scored, but is sent to the schools you are applying to as a sample of your writing skills. Admissions officers may use your essay to evaluate your writing ability when they are making admissions decisions.

Scores are released to families, and to the schools that families have designated as recipients, within 7-10 business days after the test date. Scores will be mailed to the address you provided when registering for the ISEE, and to up to six schools and/or counselors. You may request expedited score reports, or send score reports to additional schools or counselors, for an additional fee.

WHAT ARE THE ISEE PERCENTILES AND STANINES?

The ISEE score report also provides **ISEE percentile** rankings for each category, comparing your performance to that of other students in the same grade who have taken the test in the past three years. If you score in the 60th percentile, this means you are scoring higher than 60% of other students in your grade taking the exam.

These percentile rankings provide a more accurate way of evaluating student performance at each grade level. However, the ISEE percentiles are a comparison against only other students who have taken the ISEE, and these tend to be very high-achieving students. Students should not be discouraged if their percentile rankings appear low.

The following chart shows the median (50th percentile) ISEE scores for students applying to grades 5-12.

MEDIAN SCORES (ISEE 50TH PERCENTILE) FOR 2012					
Level	Grade Applying To	Verbal Reasoning	Quantitative Reasoning	Reading Comprehension	Mathematics Achievement
Lower Level	5	840	843	834	848
Lower Level	6	856	856	848	863
Middle Level	7	863	865	866	871
Middle Level	8	869	871	871	876
Upper Level	9	879	878	880	882
Upper Level	10	883	882	886	886
Upper Level	11	886	885	889	890
Upper Level	12	881	884	880	889

The ISEE score report also includes **stanine** rankings. A stanine is a number from 1-9 obtained by dividing the entire range of students' scores into 9 segments, as shown in the table below:

percentile rank	stanine
1 – 3	1
4 – 10	2
11 – 22	3
23 – 39	4
40 – 59	5
60 – 76	6
77 – 88	7

Ivy Global

89 – 95	8
96 – 99	9

Stanine scores are provided because small differences in percentile rankings may not represent a significant difference in ability. Stanines represent a range of percentile rankings, and are intended to provide a better representation of student ability.

HOW DO SCHOOLS USE THE ISEE?

Schools use the ISEE as one way to assess potential applicants, but it is by no means the only tool that they are using. Schools also pay very close attention to the rest of a student's application—academic record, teacher recommendations, extracurricular activities, writing samples, and interviews—in order to determine which students might be the best fit for their program. The personal components of a student's application sometimes give schools a lot more information about the student's personality and potential contributions to the school's overall community. Different schools place a different amount of importance on ISEE and other test scores within this process, and admissions offices are good places to find out how much your schools of interest will weight the ISEE.

Ivy Global

TEST-TAKING STRATEGIES

CHAPTER 2

APPROACHING THE ISEE

Before you review the content covered on the ISEE, you need to focus on *how* you take the ISEE. If you approach the ISEE *thoughtfully* and *strategically*, you will avoid common traps and tricks planted in the ISEE by the test makers. Think of the ISEE as a timed maze—you need to make every turn cleverly and quickly so that you avoid getting stuck at a dead end with no time to spare.

In this section, you will learn about the ISEE's format and structure; this awareness will help you avoid any surprises or shocks on test day. The ISEE is a very predictable exam and will seem less challenging once you understand what it looks like and how it works. By learning and practicing the best test-taking strategies and techniques, you will discover how to work as quickly and efficiently as possible. Once you know what to expect, you can refine your knowledge of the actual material tested on the ISEE, such as the verbal and math skills that are based on your grade level in school.

This section on ISEE strategies will answer the following **major questions**:

1. How does the ISEE differ from a test you take in school?
2. What preparation strategies can you learn before you take the ISEE?
3. What strategies can you learn to use during the ISEE?
4. How can you manage stress before and during the ISEE?

In the process of answering your big questions, this section will also highlight key facts about smart test-taking:

- Your answer choice matters—your process does not. Enter your answer choices correctly and carefully to earn points. You have a set amount of time per section, so spend it wisely.

- The ISEE's format and directions do not change, so learn them now.

- All questions have the same value.

- Each level of the ISEE corresponds to a range of grades, and score expectations differ based on your grade level.

- Identify your areas of strength and weakness, and review any content that feels unfamiliar.

- Apply universal strategies—prediction-making, Process of Elimination, back-solving, and educated guessing—to the multiple-choice sections.
- Stay calm and be confident in your abilities as you prepare for and take the ISEE.

HOW DOES THE ISEE DIFFER FROM A TEST YOU TAKE IN SCHOOL?

The ISEE differs from tests you take in school in four major ways:

1. It is not concerned with the process behind your answers. Your answer is either right or wrong: there is no partial credit.
2. You have a set amount of time per section (and for the exam as a whole).
3. It is divided into four levels that correspond to four grade ranges of students.
4. It is extremely predictable given that its format, structure, and directions never vary.

NO PARTIAL CREDIT

At this point in your school career, you have probably heard your teacher remark, "Be sure to show your work on the test!" You are most likely familiar with almost every teacher's policy of "No work, no credit." However, the ISEE completely ignores this guideline. The machine that grades your exam does not care that you penciled brilliant logic in the margins of the test booklet—the machine only looks at your answer choice. Your answer choice is either right or wrong: **there is no partial credit**.

SET AMOUNT OF TIME

You have a **set amount of time per section**, so spend it wisely. The ISEE test proctors will never award you extra time after a test section has ended because you spent half of one section struggling valiantly on a single problem. Instead, you must learn to work within each section's time constraints.

You also must view the questions as equal because **each question is worth the same number of points** (one). Even though some questions are more challenging than others, they all carry the same weight. Rather than dwell on a problem, you should skip it, work through the rest of the section, and come back to it if you have time.

FOUR LEVELS

There are four levels of the ISEE—Primary, Lower, Middle, and Upper—each of which is administered to a specific range of students. The Primary Level is given to students applying to grades 2, 3, and 4; the Lower Level is given to students applying to grades 5 and 6; the Middle Level is given to students applying to grades 7 and 8; and the Upper Level is given to students applying to grades 9, 10, 11, and 12. While you might be used to taking tests in school that are completely tailored to your grade, the ISEE is different: each test level covers content for a specific range of grade levels.

Score expectations differ based on your grade level. You are not expected to answer every question correctly on an Upper Level exam if you are only in eighth grade. Conversely, if you are in eleventh grade, you are expected to answer the most questions correctly on the Upper Level exam because you are one of the oldest students taking that exam.

STANDARD FORMAT

The ISEE is, by definition, a **standardized test**, which means that its format and directions are standard and predictable. While your teachers might change formats and directions for every assessment they administer, you can expect to see the same format and directions on every ISEE.

WHAT PREPARATION STRATEGIES CAN YOU LEARN BEFORE YOU TAKE THE ISEE?

Now that you are familiar with how the ISEE differs from the tests you take in school, you are ready to learn some test tips. You can prepare for the ISEE by following these three steps:

1. Learn the format and directions of the test.
2. Identify your areas of strength and weakness.
3. Create a study schedule to review and practice test content.

LEARN THE FORMAT AND DIRECTIONS

The structure of the ISEE is entirely predictable, so learn this now. Rather than wasting precious time reading the directions and understanding the format on test day, take the time now to familiarize yourself with the test's format and directions.

Refer to the tables on pages 6 and 7 for an overview of the ISEE's format. Continue reading for specific directions for the Verbal Reasoning, Reading Comprehension, and Essay sections. Specific directions for the Quantitative Reasoning and Mathematics Achievement sections can be found in Ivy Global's *ISEE Math*.

IDENTIFY YOUR STRENGTHS AND WEAKNESSES

To determine your areas of strength and weakness and to get an idea of which concepts you need to review, take a full-length, accurate practice exam to serve as a diagnostic test. Practice exams for the ISEE can be found in this book.

Make sure you simulate test day conditions by timing yourself. Then, check your answers against the correct answers. Write down how many questions you missed in each section, and note the topics or types of questions you found most challenging. What was hard about the test? What did you feel good about? Did you leave a lot of questions blank because of timing issues, or did you leave questions blank because you did not know how to solve them? Reflecting on these questions, in addition to looking at your score breakdown, will help you determine your strengths, weaknesses, and areas for improvement.

CREATE A STUDY SCHEDULE

After determining your areas of strength and weakness, create a study plan and schedule for your ISEE preparation to review content. Work backward from your test date until you arrive at your starting point for studying. The number of weeks you have until your exam will determine how much time you can (and should) devote to your preparation. Remember, practice is the most important thing!

To begin, try using this sample study plan as a model for your own personalized study schedule.

SAMPLE STUDY PLAN

My test date is: _____.

I have _____ weeks to study. I will make an effort to study _____ minutes/hours each night, and I will set aside extra time on _____ to take timed sections.

I plan to take _____ full-length tests between now and my test date. I will study for _____ weeks and then take a practice test. My goal for this test is to improve my score in the following sections:

_____

_____

_____

_____

_____

_____

_____

If I do not make this goal, then I will spend more time studying.

STUDY SCHEDULE				
Date	Plan of Study	Time Allotted	Time Spent	Goal Reached?
1/1	Learn 5 words and review perimeter of polygons	1 hour	44 minutes	Yes, I know 5 new words and can calculate perimeter!
1/3	Learn 5 words and review area of triangles	1 hour	1 hour	I know 5 new words, but I'm still confused about the area of triangles. I'll review this again next time and ask a teacher, tutor, or parent for help.

Ivy Global

WHAT STRATEGIES CAN YOU LEARN TO USE DURING THE TEST?

Once you have grown accustomed to the ISEE through practice, you are ready to learn strategies to use during the ISEE. The following points will prepare you to take the test as cleverly and efficiently as possible:

1. Enter your answer choices correctly and carefully.
2. Pace yourself to manage your time effectively.
3. Learn a strategic approach for multiple-choice questions.

ENTERING ANSWER CHOICES

Whether you are taking a pencil-and-paper or a computer-based exam, you must follow the directions carefully to enter your answers. In school you probably take tests that, for the most part, do not ask you to enter your answers in a specific format. However, the ISEE streamlines the grading process by only reviewing the answers you have entered on your answer sheet or into the computer program. This means that any notes or work you have written on your scratch paper will not be reviewed, and you will only receive credit for entering your answers correctly.

On a computer-based exam, you will click an answer on the computer screen in order to enter your response. Follow the directions carefully to make sure your answer has been recorded. Within each section, you will be able to go back to questions earlier in the section and change your answers. You will also be able to skip questions and come back to them later. However, you will not be able to review questions from sections that come earlier or later in the exam; you will only be able to review your answers for the questions in the section you are currently working on. Make sure all of your answers have been entered correctly before your time is up for the section.

On a pencil-and-paper exam, you will enter your answers on a separate answer sheet. You must grid in your multiple-choice answers onto this sheet using an HB pencil to fill in the circle that corresponds to your answer. This sheet is scanned and scored by a highly sensitive computer. You will also write your Essay on separate lined pages of this answer sheet.

Since you have to take an additional step to record your answers, it is important that you avoid making gridding mistakes. Sadly, many students get confused and mismark their answer sheets. Remember, even if you arrive at the right answer, it is only correct and counted in your favor if you grid correctly on your answer sheet.

To grid correctly and carefully to maximize your points, consider the following tips:

Keep your answer sheet neat. Since your answer sheet is graded by a machine, your score is calculated based on what your marks look like. The machine cannot know what you really meant if you picked the wrong bubble. Stray marks can harm your score, especially if you darken the correct answer but accidentally make a mark that confuses the machine! Avoid this and other errors by consulting the following image, which shows the difference between answers that are properly shaded and those that are not.

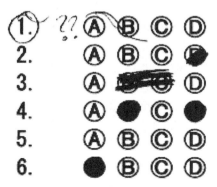

Answer 1 is *wrong* because no answer is selected and there are stray marks.
Answer 2 is *wrong* because choice (D) has not been darkened completely.
Answer 3 is *wrong* because two answers have been partially selected.
Answer 4 is *wrong* because two answers have been selected.
Answer 5 is *neither right nor wrong* because it was left blank.
Answer 6 is *right* because choice (A) has been darkened properly.

Train yourself to **circle your answer choice in your test booklet**. If you have time to go back and check your answers, you can easily check your circled answers against your gridded ones.

You should also **create a system for marking questions that you skipped** or that you found confusing (see the next section for more information about skipping questions). Try circling those question numbers only in your test booklet so that you can find them later if you want to solve them or check your work. Be aware of these questions when gridding answers on your answer sheet.

Finally, **grid your answers in batches of four, five, or six answer choices.** That way, you do not have to go back and forth between your test booklet and your answer sheet every minute. If you choose to use this strategy, keep an eye on the clock—you do not want to get to the end of the section and find you have not gridded any answers. Depending on how much time you have left to check your work (if you happen to finish early), you can either review every problem or spot-check a series of questions on your answer sheet against your test booklet.

TIME MANAGEMENT (PACING)

Manage your time effectively to boost your score. The ISEE has an element of time pressure, so it is important to keep moving on the exam rather than spending too much time on any single question.

You can come back to questions within each section of the ISEE. Each question is only worth one point, regardless of its difficulty. If you are stuck on a problem, you should make your best guess and move on to try to answer another problem. It makes more sense to answer as many questions as possible (and get as many points as possible) rather than spending all your time on one question. If you come across a question you want to come back to, circle it in your question booklet or mark it on your scratch paper. Remember not to make any stray marks on your answer sheet.

By moving quickly through each question of the section, you will ensure that: 1) you see every question in the section; 2) you gain points on questions that are easy for you; 3) you return to more challenging problems and figure out as many as you can with your remaining time. It is also important to note that you might not be able to answer several questions in each section if you are on the younger end of the testing group for your particular test level. In that case, you should make your best guess based on the information you do know, but shouldn't worry if the content is unfamiliar.

Even if you are unsure about a question and want to come back to it later, you should **always make a guess.** The ISEE doesn't take off any points for answering questions incorrectly, so you should never leave a question blank! Even if you guess a completely random answer, you have a small chance of gaining a point. If you can rule out one or two choices that you know are wrong, you have even better odds of guessing the right answer. Therefore, always make a guess on every question, even if you are planning to come back to it later. When your time is up, you want to make sure that you have entered an answer for every question!

Follow this step-by-step process for moving through a section:

1. Look through the section and answer the questions that are easy for you. If a question seems difficult or is taking too long, make a guess and circle it to come back to later.

2. After answering all the easier questions, go back to the questions you have circled and spend some time working on ones that you think you might be able to solve. If you figure out that the answer you originally guessed was incorrect, change that answer on your answer sheet.

3. If you have no idea how to solve a question, leave your best guess as your answer.

4. If you have any time remaining, check your work for the questions you solved.

STRATEGIES FOR MULTIPLE-CHOICE QUESTIONS

Apply universal strategies—prediction-making, Process of Elimination, back-solving, and educated guessing—to the multiple-choice sections. To illustrate the value of these strategies, read through the following example of a synonym question from the Verbal Reasoning section:

HAPPY:

(A) delighted

(B) unhappy

(C) crazy

(D) nice

Answer: (A). "Delighted" is the correct answer because it is the word that most nearly means "happy."

Regardless of whether the answer choices are easy, difficult, or somewhere in between, you can use certain tricks and tips to your advantage. To approach ISEE questions effectively, you need to step into the test makers' minds and learn to avoid their traps.

Make predictions. When you see a question, try to come up with an answer on your own before looking at the answer choices. You can literally cover the answer choices with your hand so that you must rely on your own intelligence to predict an answer instead of being swayed by answer choices that you see. If you look at the answer choices first, you might be tempted to pick an answer without thinking about the other options and what the question is asking you. Instead, make a prediction so that you understand the question fully and get a clear sense of what to look for in the answers. In the synonym example above, you could predict that a possible synonym for "happy" would be something like "glad."

Use the Process of Elimination. For each multiple-choice question, you must realize that the answer is right in front of you. To narrow down your answer choices, think about the potential incorrect answers and actively identify those to eliminate them. Even if you can eliminate just one answer, you will set yourself up for better odds if you decide to guess. For the synonym example above, test your prediction of "glad" against the answer choices and immediately eliminate "unhappy" since it is opposite in meaning. You can also probably eliminate "crazy" and "nice" since those words do not match your prediction. This leaves you with "delighted," which is the correct answer.

Try back-solving. This strategy is most useful on the math sections, especially when you are given a complicated, multi-step word problem. Instead of writing an equation, try plugging in the answer choices to the word problem. Take a look at the following question:

Catherine has a basket of candy. On Monday, she eats ½ of all the candy. On Tuesday, she eats 2 pieces. On Wednesday, she eats twice the amount of candy that she consumed on Tuesday. If she only has 4 pieces left on Thursday, how many pieces did she initially have?

(A) 12
(B) 14
(C) 16
(D) 20

To use back-solving, start with answer choice (C) and plug it into the word problem. If (C) is the correct answer, you are done. If not, you will then know whether you should test (B) or (D). When we start with 16 pieces of candy, we subtract 8 on Monday, then 2 more for Tuesday, and then 4 more for Wednesday. By Thursday, Catherine only has two pieces of candy left, which is less than the amount we wanted. Therefore, we know our answer has to be bigger, so we eliminate choices (A), (B), and (C) and try (D), which works.

(*Fun Fact:* If you think about it, you will have to plug in three answer choices at most to determine the right answer.)

Armed with these strategies, you might feel that the ISEE is starting to look more manageable because you now have shortcuts that will help you navigate the maze of questions quickly and cleverly.

Take a look at this example to practice using the strategies you just read about.

Because Kaitlin was -------- from her soccer game, she went to bed early.

(A) thrilled
(B) exhausted
(C) competitive
(D) inspired

1. Assess the question and recognize what it is testing. In this case, the question tests whether you can pick a word to complete the sentence.
2. Make a prediction. What about Kaitlin's soccer game would cause her to go to bed early? Maybe it wore her out, so we could look for something like "tired" to go in the blank.
3. Look for inaccurate answer choices and eliminate them. If Kaitlin were "thrilled," "competitive," or "inspired" as a result of her soccer game, this wouldn't explain why she had to go to bed early. Therefore, you can eliminate answers (A), (C), and (D).

4. Make an educated guess, or choose the answer you feel most confident about. Since you made a fantastic prediction and used Process of Elimination, you only have one choice left: (B). "Exhausted" is the correct answer—you just earned yourself a point!

HOW CAN YOU MANAGE YOUR STRESS?

If you have ever taken a big test before, or had an important sports match, play, or presentation, then you know what anxiety feels like. Even if you are excited for an approaching event, you might feel nervous. You might begin to doubt yourself, and you might feel as if your mind is racing while butterflies flutter in your stomach!

When it comes to preparing for the ISEE, the good news is that a little anxiety (or adrenaline) goes a long way. Anxiety is a natural, motivating force that will help you study hard in the days leading up to your test. That anxiety will also help you stay alert and work efficiently during the test.

Sometimes, however, anxiety might become larger than life and start to get the best of you. To prevent anxiety and nerves from clouding your ability to work effectively and believe in yourself, you should try some of the suggestions below. Many of these suggestions are good ideas to use in everyday life, but they become especially important in the final week before your test and on test day itself.

- **Relax and slow down.** To center yourself and ease your anxiety, take a big, deep breath. Slowly inhale for a few seconds and then slowly exhale for a few seconds. Shut your eyes and relax. Stretch your arms, roll your neck gently, crack your knuckles—get in the zone of Zen! Continue to breathe deeply and slowly until you can literally feel your body calm down.
- **Picture your goals.** Close your eyes or just pause to reflect on what you want to achieve on test day. Visualize your success, whether that means simply answering all the math questions or getting a top score and gaining acceptance into the school of your dreams. Acknowledge your former successes and abilities, and believe in yourself.
- **Break it down.** Instead of trying to study a whole section at once, break up your studying into small and manageable chunks. Outline your study goals before you start. For example, instead of trying to master the entire Reading Comprehension section at once, you might want to work on one type of passage at a time.
- **Sleep.** Make sure you get plenty of rest and sleep, especially the two nights leading up to your exam!
- **Fuel up.** Eat healthy, filling meals that fuel your brain. Also, drink lots of water to stay hydrated.
- **Take a break.** Put down the books and go play outside, read, listen to music, exercise, or have a good conversation with friend or family member. A good break can be just as restful as a nap. However, watching television will provide minimal relaxation.

On the night before the exam, study only lightly. Make a list of your three biggest fears and work on them, but don't try to learn anything new. Pick out what you are going to wear to the exam—try wearing layers in case the exam room is hotter or colder than you expect. Organize everything you need to bring. Know where the test center is located and how long it will take to get there. Have a nutritious meal and get plenty of sleep!

On the morning of the exam, let your adrenaline kick in naturally. Eat a good breakfast and stay hydrated; your body needs fuel to endure the test. Bring along several pencils and a good eraser. Listen carefully to the test proctor's instructions and let the proctor know if you are left-handed so you can sit at an appropriate desk. Take a deep breath and remember: you are smart and accomplished! Believe in yourself and you will do just fine.

PRACTICE TESTS

CHAPTER 3

PRACTICE TEST 1

LOWER LEVEL

HOW TO TAKE THIS PRACTICE TEST

To simulate an accurate testing environment, sit at a desk in a quiet location free of distractions—no TV, computers, phones, music, or noise—and clear your desk of all materials except pencils and erasers. Remember that no calculators, rulers, protractors, dictionaries, or other aids are allowed on the ISEE.

Give yourself the following amounts of time for each section:

SECTION	SUBJECT	TIME LIMIT
1	Verbal Reasoning	20 minutes
2	Quantitative Reasoning	35 minutes
5 minute break		
3	Reading Comprehension	25 minutes
4	Mathematics Achievement	30 minutes
5 minute break		
5	Essay	30 minutes

Have an adult help you monitor your time, or use a watch and time yourself. Only give yourself the allotted time for each section; put your pencil down when your time is up.

Follow the instructions carefully. As you take your test, bubble your answers into the answer sheets provided. Use the test booklet as scratch paper for notes and calculations. Remember that you are not granted time at the end of a section to transfer your answers to the answer sheet, so you must do this as you go along.

When you are finished, check your answers against the answer keys provided. Then, score your exam using the directions at the end of the book.

Ivy Global

Section 1
Verbal Reasoning

34 Questions   **Time: 20 minutes**

This section is divided into two parts that contain two different types of questions. As soon as you have completed Part One, answer the questions in Part Two. You may write in your test booklet. For each answer you select, fill in the corresponding circle on your answer document.

PART ONE — SYNONYMS

Each question in Part One consists of a word in capital letters followed by four answer choices. Select the one word that is most nearly the same in meaning as the word in capital letters.

SAMPLE QUESTION: Sample Answer

    CHARGE: Ⓐ Ⓑ ● Ⓓ

    (A) release

    (B) belittle

    (C) accuse

    (D) conspire

The correct answer is "accuse," so circle C is darkened.

Go on to the next page ➡

VR

PART TWO — SENTENCE COMPLETION

Each question in Part Two is made up of a sentence with one blank. Each blank indicates that a word or phrase is missing. The sentence is followed by four answer choices. Select the word or phrase that will best complete the meaning of the sentence as a whole.

SAMPLE QUESTIONS:

<u>Sample Answer</u>

It rained so much that the streets were -------.

● Ⓑ Ⓒ Ⓓ

(A) flooded

(B) arid

(C) paved

(D) crowded

The correct answer is "flooded," so circle A is darkened.

Ⓐ Ⓑ Ⓒ ●

The house was so dirty that it took -------.

(A) less than ten minutes to wash it.

(B) four months to demolish it.

(C) over a week to walk across it.

(D) two days to clean it.

The correct answer is "two days to clean it," so circle D is darkened.

STOP. Do not go on until told to do so.

PART ONE – SYNONYMS

Directions: Select the word that is most nearly the same in meaning as the word in capital letters.

1. DENIAL
   (A) flow
   (B) lie
   (C) rejection
   (D) encouragement

2. SIMPLE
   (A) boring
   (B) silent
   (C) plain
   (D) nice

3. QUAKE
   (A) stake
   (B) fall
   (C) slam
   (D) shake

4. SIGNAL
   (A) obscure
   (B) assail
   (C) indicate
   (D) assume

5. AUTHORIZE
   (A) approve
   (B) demand
   (C) replenish
   (D) attempt

6. YIELD
   (A) imply
   (B) avoid
   (C) announce
   (D) surrender

7. HERALD
   (A) dance
   (B) announce
   (C) protect
   (D) insult

8. TRUCE
   (A) pine
   (B) tractor
   (C) declaration
   (D) ceasefire

9. SEVERITY
   (A) harshness
   (B) drought
   (C) division
   (D) wound

10. SAGE
    (A) spicy
    (B) ancient
    (C) false
    (D) wise

Go on to the next page ➡

11. RESTRAINT

(A) reserve

(B) pressure

(C) repetition

(D) rescue

12. WARBLE

(A) trip

(B) worry

(C) assail

(D) sing

13. RECOIL

(A) escape

(B) braid

(C) unbind

(D) withdraw

14. ENVELOP

(A) enclose

(B) entrust

(C) freeze

(D) inside

15. CREED

(A) belief

(B) avarice

(C) guilt

(D) admiration

16. IMMUNITY

(A) disrespect

(B) resistance

(C) ability

(D) dirtiness

17. FORLORN

(A) short

(B) evil

(C) lonely

(D) hidden

Go on to the next page ➡

PART TWO – SENTENCE COMPLETION

Directions: Select the word that best completes the sentence.

18. Seeing that the conditions were ----------
for surfing, Liya quickly grabbed her
wetsuit.

    (A) insufficient

    (B) faulty

    (C) ideal

    (D) honest

19. Mazen left his cake in the oven too long,
but he hoped he could ---------- it by
covering it with icing.

    (A) salvage

    (B) secure

    (C) escape

    (D) measure

20. The nature guide always warns hikers not
to touch any snakes that they ---------- on
the trail, as many local species are
poisonous.

    (A) elude

    (B) oppose

    (C) reject

    (D) encounter

21. The new book received ---------- reviews
for its meticulous coverage, high-quality
illustrations, and engaging discussion.

    (A) calm

    (B) negative

    (C) moveable

    (D) favorable

22. Joan travelled to Thailand, where she
learned to prepare ---------- Pad Thai
from traditional chefs.

    (A) artificial

    (B) authentic

    (C) distressing

    (D) useless

23. Scientists in Brazil were ------------ when
they discovered a new species of river
dolphin.

    (A) thrilled

    (B) eager

    (C) dejected

    (D) bored

24. When Maya learned that Tommy played
piano, ran track and field, and
volunteered with seniors, she was
impressed by the ---------- of his interests.

    (A) increase

    (B) resemblance

    (C) variety

    (D) community

25. Charlie Chaplin was a British comic actor,
filmmaker, and composer who rose to
---------- in the silent era.

    (A) prominence

    (B) elevation

    (C) dependence

    (D) creation

Go on to the next page ➡

26. Wujie was ----------- when his class was cancelled, because it gave him more time to complete important homework.

    (A) disappointed

    (B) relieved

    (C) confused

    (D) aggravated

27. Sainte-Enimie, in southern France, is the location of several monasteries and other interesting ----------- sites.

    (A) mundane

    (B) religious

    (C) offensive

    (D) theoretical

28. Sheep's wool is the most widely used animal fiber, and is usually ----------- by shearing.

    (A) planted

    (B) concluded

    (C) dispersed

    (D) harvested

29. John knew a healthy diet called for a variety of vegetables, but -----------.

    (A) he ate numerous kinds.

    (B) he enjoyed many kinds of fruit.

    (C) he only ate spinach.

    (D) he was adept at preparing desserts.

30. Although the author claimed her work was pure fiction, those who knew her well -----------.

    (A) recognized many real events from her life.

    (B) bought several copies.

    (C) did not understand it.

    (D) supported her career as a writer.

31. Since she was a skilled surgeon, Dr. Gavora -----------.

    (A) had a passion for skiing.

    (B) successfully performed the operation.

    (C) enjoyed watching foreign films.

    (D) had been interested in medicine from a young age.

32. Jolie had been looking forward to the recital, but she -----------.

    (A) bought new shoes for the occasion.

    (B) fell ill and was unable to perform.

    (C) was planning to perform her favorite song.

    (D) knew how to play in a variety of musical styles.

33. In contrast to the realistic and conventional style of his early paintings, Pablo Picasso's later work in the Cubist style -----------.

    (A) was not well known by critics.

    (B) looked very life-like and natural.

    (C) was far more abstract and experimental.

    (D) was not popular, causing him to lose money.

34. Ceres was the first asteroid ever discovered, but -----------.

    (A) researchers initially thought it was a planet.

    (B) researchers study objects in space.

    (C) there are many different types of asteroids.

    (D) telescopes have become more powerful in recent years.

STOP. Do not go on until told to do so.

Section 2
Quantitative Reasoning

38 Questions	Time: 35 minutes

Each question is followed by four suggested answers. Read each question and then decide which one of the four suggested answers is best.

Find the row of spaces on your answer document that has the same number as the question. In this row, mark the space having the same letter as the answer you have chosen. You may write in your test booklet.

SAMPLE QUESTIONS: <u>Sample Answer</u>

What is the value of the expression $(4 + 6) \div 2$?   Ⓐ Ⓑ ● Ⓓ

(A) 2

(B) 4

(C) 5

(D) 7

The correct answer is 5, so circle C is darkened.

A square has an area of 25cm². What is the length of one of its   Ⓐ ● Ⓒ Ⓓ
sides?

(A) 1 cm

(B) 5 cm

(C) 10 cm

(D) 25 cm

The correct answer is 5 so circle B is darkened.

STOP. Do not go on until told to do so.   **STOP**

1. The large square shown below has been divided into smaller squares.

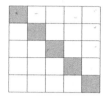

What fraction of the large square is shaded?

(A) $^5/_5$

(B) $^1/_2$

(C) $^1/_3$

(D) $^1/_5$

2. Which expression is equivalent to the expression $(2 + 3) \div 4$?

(A) $5 + 4$

(B) 5×4

(C) $\frac{2}{3} + 4$

(D) $5 \times \frac{1}{4}$

3. Four students were asked to walk, jog, and sprint around a track. Every two minutes, their speeds were recorded in the table below.

Times	Walking Student	Jogging Student	Sprinting Student
2 min	5.00 km/hr	11.50 km/hr	20.00 km/hr
4 min	5.00 km/hr	11.00 km/hr	16.00 km/hr
6 min	5.00 km/hr	10.50 km/hr	14.00 km/hr
8 min	5.00 km/hr	10.00 km/hr	13.00 km/hr

According to the pattern in this table, what would be the predicted speed of the sprinting student at 10 minutes?

(A) 14.00 km/hr

(B) 12.50 km/hr

(C) 10.00 km/hr

(D) 8.50 km/hr

Go on to the next page ➡

4. Which story best suits the equation $21 \div 7 = 3$?

(A) Susie has 21 pieces of gum that she wants to share equally between her 7 friends. How many pieces of gum does she give each friend?

(B) Susie had 21 pieces of gum and ate 7. How many pieces of gum did she have left?

(C) Susie has 21 packs of gum, each with 7 pieces. How many pieces of gum does Susie have?

(D) Susie has 21 pieces of gum and gives 3 packs of gum to her friend. How many packs of gum does Susie have left?

5. Use the number line to answer the question.

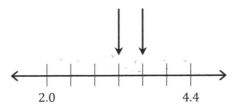

What values are the arrows pointing to?

(A) 2.3, 2.4

(B) 2.8, 3.2

(C) 3.2, 3.6

(D) 4.0, 4.1

6. Which is the smallest fraction?

(A) $^2/_3$

(B) $^{14}/_{30}$

(C) $^4/_7$

(D) $^5/_{10}$

7. Which equation can be read as "4 less than half a number is equal to 2 more than the number?" Let a represent the unknown number.

(A) $(a - 4) \times \frac{1}{2} = 2 + a$

(B) $a + \frac{1}{2} - 4 = a - 2$

(C) $a \div 2 + 4 = 2 - a$

(D) $\frac{a}{2} - 4 = a + 2$

8. Use the pattern to help answer the question.

X X O, X X X O, X X X X O, ...

Which comes next?

(A) X X X X X X X O

(B) O X X X X X O

(C) O X X X X X

(D) X X X X X O

9. Andrea and Zach walk home together after school at a constant speed of 13 kilometers per hour. Zach's house is three times farther from school than Andrea's house. If it takes Zach 33 minutes to walk home, how long does it take Andrea to walk home?

(A) 11 minutes

(B) 13 minutes

(C) 39 minutes

(D) 66 minutes

10. Jeff is thinking of a prime number between 1 and 20. Jeff says that the number is greater than 11 and less than 17. What number is Jeff thinking of?

(A) 11

(B) 12

(C) 13

(D) 15

Go on to the next page ➡

11. A survey of 32 artists' favorite colors is displayed in the circle graph below.

Artists' Favorite Colors

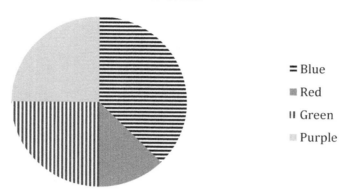

= Blue

▦ Red

‖ Green

▦ Purple

Approximately what fraction of the artists chose blue as their favorite color?

(A) $^1/_8$

(B) $^1/_4$

(C) $^2/_7$

(D) $^3/_8$

---

12. The triangle below has an area of A inches. If the formula for the area of a triangle is $area = \frac{1}{2}base \times height$, which equation would tell you the length of the triangle's base in inches?

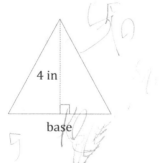

4 in

base

(A) base $= A \div 2$

(B) base $= A \times 2$

(C) base $= A \times 2 - 4$

(D) base $= A \div 4 + 4$

13. Use the equations to answer the question.

$$4a = 8$$
$$2 + b = 3$$

What is the sum of a and b?

(A) 1

(B) 2

(C) 3

(D) 6

Go on to the next page ➡

14. Use the diagram to answer the question.

Which piece would complete the diagram to make a square?

(A)

(B)

(C)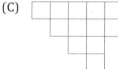

(D)

15. Use the following equation to answer the question.

$$p \times 15 = q$$

By which number can q be divided without leaving a remainder?

(A) 2

(B) 3

(C) 4

(D) 10

16. Lucy has a bag full of marbles of various colors. The probability of choosing a red marble is 5 out of 12. Which combination of marbles is possible?

(A) 5 red marbles and 12 others

(B) 15 red marbles and 36 others

(C) 24 red marbles and 10 others

(D) 20 red marbles and 28 others

17. For which pair of symbols below do both symbols have the same number of lines of symmetry?

(A) ⚹ ♈

(B) ⊘ ○

(C) ★ ✸

(D) △ ⚡

18. Use the Venn diagram to answer the question.

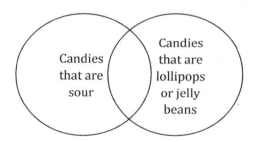

What candy could be found in the overlapping area of the Venn diagram?

(A) A sugary lollipop

(B) A sour jelly bean

(C) A sugary jelly bean

(D) A sour piece of gum

Go on to the next page ➡

19. The figure below shows Julie's juice box after she drank some of the juice.

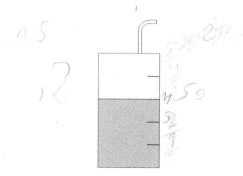

Julie has 150 mL of juice left. If the juice box was completely full before she started drinking, how much juice did Julie drink?

(A) 250 mL

(B) 200 mL

(C) 150 mL

(D) 100 mL

20. Use the table to determine the rule.

Input	Output
●	✧
1	0
2	3
4	9
10	27
26	75

What is the rule for the function?

(A) ● + 3 − 3 = ✧

(B) 3● − 3 = ✧

(C) ● × 2 + 7 = ✧

(D) 4● − 1 = ✧

21. Rachel has four bags of candy. Two of the bags weigh $3\frac{1}{2}$ lb, one bag weighs 4 lb, and one bag weighs 5 lb. What is the mean weight of all four bags?

(A) 4 lb

(B) $4\frac{1}{4}$ lb

(C) $4\frac{3}{8}$ lb

(D) $4\frac{1}{2}$ lb

22. The perimeter of a square is 16w. What is the length of one side?

(A) 4

(B) 8

(C) 4w

(D) 8w

23. The length of AB is x, the length of BC is y, and the length of BD is z.

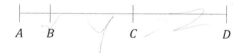

What is the length of AD?

(A) $x + y + z$

(B) $x - y + z$

(C) yz

(D) $x + z$

24. Use the two equations below to answer the question:

$$3 ● + 2 ☺ = 18$$
$$☺ = 3$$

What is the value of ●?

(A) 2

(B) 3

(C) 4

(D) 5

Go on to the next page ➡

25. Use the figure below to answer the question.

If the length and the width of the figure were both increased by two units, what would be the new perimeter of the figure?

(A) 22 units

(B) 26 units

(C) 28 units

(D) 42 units

26. What is the value of b in the expression below?

$$\frac{16 \times 48 \div 24}{8} = b$$

(A) 2

(B) 4

(C) 6

(D) 8

27. Leslie bought 416 erasers for $0.27 each. Which expression gives the best estimate of the total amount of money she spent?

(A) $42 \div 3$

(B) 41×27

(C) 400×0.3

(D) 300×2.7

28. 8 small boxes can fit into a larger rectangular box. One of the small boxes is shown inside the large rectangular box below.

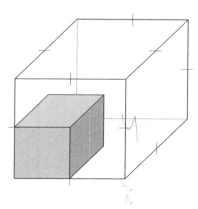

The volume of the large rectangular box is 16 units³. What is the volume of each small box?

(A) 1 units³

(B) 2 units³

(C) 4 units³

(D) 64 units³

29. Sam has a bag with 18 pieces of chocolate, gummies, and mints. There are three times as many chocolates as there are gummies, and twice as many gummies as there are mints. How many mints does Sam have?

(A) 6

(B) 4

(C) 2

(D) 1

Go on to the next page ➡

Ivy Global

30. Rushen had three bottles of soda. Each bottle contained two liters of soda, and she divided the soda equally into 20 glasses for her friends. How much soda did she pour into each glass?

    (A) $\frac{1}{10}$ L

    (B) $\frac{3}{10}$ L

    (C) $\frac{1}{2}$ L

    (D) 6 L

31. Kim's house is 11 km from Joe's house. On a map, this distance is represented by 5.75 cm. How many centimeters would represent 66 km on the map?

    (A) 30 cm

    (B) 34.5 cm

    (C) 40.75 cm

    (D) 52 cm

32. Use the figure shown to answer the question.

    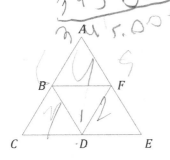

    Lucy wants to use the figure above to draw different quadrilaterals. She can only trace the straight lines connecting the points *A*, *B*, *C*, *D*, *E*, and *F*. How many quadrilaterals can she draw?

    (A) 0

    (B) 3

    (C) 4

    (D) 6

33. Alex did the problem shown with his calculator.

    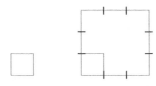

    $$\frac{27 \times 189}{59}$$

    What is a reasonable estimation for his answer?

    (A) between 50 and 150

    (B) between 150 and 250

    (C) between 500 and 1,500

    (D) between 1,500 and 2,500

34. How many small unit squares would you need to build a larger square where each side has a length of 3 unit squares?

    unit square   larger square

    (A) 3

    (B) 8

    (C) 9

    (D) 12

35. Use the number line shown to answer the question.

    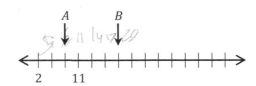

    The value of *B* is the difference between another number and *A*. What is the other number?

    (A) 28

    (B) 20

    (C) 8

    (D) 2

Go on to the next page ➡

36. Five students timed how long it takes them to walk to school and recorded the data in the graph shown below.

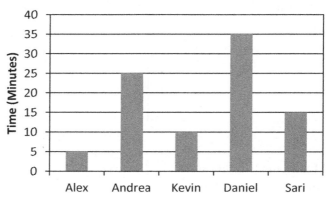

Time Spent Walking to School

Which of the following statements is correct?

(A) The mean (average) walking time is between 25 and 35 minutes

(B) It takes Andrea twice as long to walk to school as it does Kevin.

(C) The range of the data is greater than the number of minutes it takes Andrea to walk to school.

(D) It takes Daniel longer to walk to school than all of the other students combined.

---

37. The perimeter of the shape below is 16.5 inches.

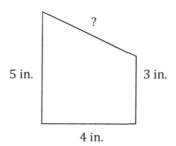

5 in.   ?   3 in.

4 in.

What is the length of the missing side?

(A) 6 in.

(B) 4.5 in.

(C) 3.5 in.

(D) 2 in.

38. Eloise flips a two-sided coin 100 times. The coin has an equal probability of landing on the "heads" side or landing on the "tails" side, and Eloise records which side it lands on after each flip. Which of the following most likely resembles Eloise's results?

(A) 94 heads, 6 tails

(B) 100 heads, 100 tails

(C) 47 heads, 53 tails

(D) 0 heads, 100 tails

STOP. Do not go on until told to do so.

Ivy Global

Section 3
Reading Comprehension

| 25 Questions | Time: 25 minutes |

This section contains five short reading passages. Each passage is followed by five questions based on its content. Answer the questions following each passage on the basis of what is <u>stated</u> or <u>implied</u> in that passage. You may write in your test booklet.

STOP. Do not go on
until told to do so.

Questions 1–5

1 I remember from my childhood an
2 occasion on which my teacher enthusiastically
3 announced to the class that we would be going
4 on a field trip. While a field trip is always
5 welcome news, I wasn't thrilled about our
6 destination: we were going to visit some
7 ancient earthen mounds. Our teacher informed
8 us that the mounds pre-dated the pyramids of
9 Egypt. She told us that when European
10 explorers first encountered the mounds, the
11 people living in the region had no memory of
12 when they were built or who built them. She
13 read with us about the lost people who built
14 them and also built cities thousands of years
15 before the arrival of European settlers in North
16 America.
17 Just the month before, my brother's class
18 had gone to a zoo! As much as our teacher tried
19 to instill in us a sense of the historical
20 significance of the site we were going to visit,
21 observing large piles of old dirt still seemed
22 less exciting than spending a day gawking at
23 exotic animals and buying treats from carts. It
24 was difficult for me not to feel as though this
25 was going to be a second-rate field trip, and on
26 the long bus ride I thought mainly of how much
27 more fun a trip the zoo would have been.
28 But when we arrived, I couldn't help but
29 be affected by the mounds. As we walked
30 among them and our guide described the lives
31 of the people whose bodies were now interred
32 within them, I felt the weight of their history as
33 I had not when I had been only reading about
34 it. History transformed from a collection of
35 facts to real human experience: people had
36 been there, and they lived, grew up, grew old,
37 and died. Their cities dissolved, and they had
38 been almost completely forgotten, but their
39 works left a mark in history—and thousands of
40 years later, we were learning their stories. It
41 was a haunting and humbling experience. On
42 the ride home, I didn't think of the zoo at all.

Go on to the next page ➡

1. The author's main purpose in this passage is to

   (A) describe an ancient civilization.

   (B) express an opinion about earthen mounds.

   (C) explain why she has never been to a zoo.

   (D) tell a story about a field trip.

2. As it is used in the passage, the word "interred" (line 31) most nearly means

   (A) in-between.

   (B) buried.

   (C) entered.

   (D) studied.

3. In the second paragraph (lines 17-27), the narrator's attitude as a child could best be described as

   (A) rational.

   (B) joyful.

   (C) enthusiastic.

   (D) pessimistic.

4. With which of the following statements would the author most likely agree?

   (A) A field trip to the zoo would have been better than the field trip to the mounds.

   (B) Reading too much about your destination in advance can ruin the experience of a field trip.

   (C) Tour guides are usually better at teaching than classroom teachers are.

   (D) Some lessons are easier to learn through experience than by just reading about them.

5. According to information in the passage, the earthen mounds were

   (A) even more ancient than the pyramids in Egypt.

   (B) built by European explorers, but later forgotten.

   (C) similar in construction to the pyramids in Egypt.

   (D) built in the first North American cities.

Go on to the next page ➡

Questions 6–10

1   Fireflies are common insects found
2 throughout temperate and tropical
3 environments. These insects are well-known
4 for a light that they produce using a chemical
5 reaction. Many of us have seen fireflies lighting
6 up the night-time air in parks and open fields,
7 or have even tried to catch them in order to
8 watch them glow up close.
9   These flying adult fireflies are most likely
10 using their glow in order to attract mates. In
11 many species, the male firefly creates flashes of
12 light while flying around an area, and then the
13 female responds to these aerial flashes with a
14 flash of her own. These mating behaviors vary
15 between species of firefly, however. In some
16 species, only the female adult flashes, and in
17 other species, only the males flash. In some
18 species, neither the male nor the female
19 flashes, and the fireflies instead use scent to
20 find mates.

21   Firefly larvae also glow, and for this
22 reason they are sometimes known as
23 glowworms. Larvae are the young form of
24 fireflies, and all firefly larvae glow, even in
25 species in which the adult fireflies do not glow.
26 This glowing is not intended to attract mates,
27 but is more likely intended to warn potential
28 predators against eating the young insects.
29 Most glowworms have a bad taste or may even
30 be poisonous to eat.
31   There are also some fireflies that use
32 their glow for another purpose altogether:
33 predation. In these species of firefly, the female
34 uses her flash to mimic the flash of a female of
35 another species. When males of the other
36 species are attracted by the flash, the predatory
37 females kill and eat them. This has earned
38 these fireflies the nickname "femme fatale."

Go on to the next page ➡

6. The primary purpose of this passage is to

   (A) disprove popular myths about fireflies.

   (B) describe several types of glowing insects.

   (C) provide information about various types of fireflies.

   (D) explain that certain fireflies use their glow to attract prey.

7. Based on information in the passage, we can infer that fireflies are probably

   (A) the only type of insect that uses a chemical reaction to glow.

   (B) larger and more complex than most flying insects.

   (C) found in many different places throughout the world.

   (D) more common in tropical environments than temperate ones.

8. Which question could be answered with information from the passage?

   (A) Are some fireflies predators?

   (B) Why don't all fireflies have the ability to glow as adults?

   (C) Which species of firefly is most common?

   (D) In what part of the world were fireflies first discovered?

9. According to the passage, glowworms are

   (A) a type of worm with similar traits to fireflies.

   (B) the only species of firefly that doesn't fly.

   (C) a predatory type of firefly.

   (D) the young form of any species of firefly.

10. In line 13, "aerial" most nearly means

    (A) in the air.

    (B) brighter than usual.

    (C) predatory.

    (D) warning.

Go on to the next page ➡

Questions 11–15

1   Chaji is a Japanese tea ceremony. The
2 guests arrive early and enter an interior
3 waiting room, where they leave their coats and
4 other possessions and put on fresh tabi—
5 special socks worn with traditional Japanese
6 sandals. The waiting room is decorated with a
7 hanging scroll which has artwork or writing on
8 it, and which usually has a seasonal theme.
9 When all the guests have arrived and finished
10 their preparations, they go to an outdoor
11 waiting bench in a simple garden outside the
12 teahouse, where they remain until summoned
13 by the host.
14   Following a silent bow between host and
15 guests, the guests take turns going to a stone
16 basin where they ritually purify themselves by
17 washing their hands and rinsing their mouths
18 with water. They remove their sandals and
19 enter the tea room, where they sit on mats.
20 Here, too, there is a hanging scroll.
21   In cool months, a fire is made at the
22 beginning of the chaji, before the meal. In
23 warmer months, the fire is not made until after
24 the meal. The meal includes several courses
25 accompanied by rice wine and followed by a
26 small sweet. After the meal there is a break,
27 during which the guests return to the garden
28 while the host replaces the scroll with a flower
29 arrangement, opens the tea room's shutters,
30 and makes preparations for serving the tea.

Go on to the next page ➡

11. This passage is primarily about Japanese

    (A) manners.

    (B) food.

    (C) tea ceremonies.

    (D) gardens.

12. According to the passage, the guests at a Japanese tea ceremony remove their sandals

    (A) before entering the waiting room.

    (B) before entering the garden.

    (C) before entering the tea room.

    (D) before washing their hands.

13. The mood of a Japanese tea ceremony could best be described as

    (A) tense.

    (B) casual.

    (C) dark.

    (D) formal.

14. It can be inferred from the passage that during the meal

    (A) the host is not present.

    (B) the guests eat too much.

    (C) the host gets very tired.

    (D) the shutters of the tea room are shut.

15. As it is used in line 16, "purify" most nearly means

    (A) clean.

    (B) finish.

    (C) observe.

    (D) dabble.

Go on to the next page ➡

Questions 16–20

1   It was a hot morning late in July when
2   the school opened. I trembled when I heard the
3   patter of little feet down the dusty road and
4   saw the growing row of dark solemn faces and
5   bright eager eyes facing me.
6   There they sat, nearly thirty of them, on
7   the rough benches, their faces shading from a
8   pale cream to a deep brown, the little feet bare
9   and swinging, the eyes full of expectation, with
10 here and there a twinkle of mischief, and the
11 hands grasping Webster's blue-back spelling-
12 book. I loved my school, and the fine faith the
13 children had in the wisdom of their teacher
14 was truly marvelous. We read and spelled
15 together, wrote a little, picked flowers, sang,
16 and listened to stories of the world beyond the
17 hill.

18 At times the school would dwindle away,
19 and I would start out. I would visit the Eddings,
20 who lived in two very dirty rooms, and ask why
21 little Lugene, whose flaming face seemed ever
22 ablaze with the dark-red hair uncombed, was
23 absent all last week, or why the unmistakable
24 rags of Mack and Ed were so often missing.
25 Then their father would tell me how the crops
26 needed the boys, and their mother would
27 assure me that Lugene must mind the baby.
28 "But we'll start them again next week." When
29 the Lawrences stopped, I knew that the doubts
30 of the old folks about book-learning had
31 conquered again, and so, toiling up the hill, I
32 put Cicero's "pro Archia Poeta" into the
33 simplest English, and usually convinced
34 them—for a week or so.

Go on to the next page ➡

16. How did the speaker feel about his job at the school?

    (A) He enjoyed having such easy and entertaining work.

    (B) He resented the fact that his students didn't appreciate his expertise.

    (C) He was bored by the simple activities he had to engage in with his students.

    (D) He was proud of his school and worked hard to maintain it.

17. According to the passage, when school attendance was low the speaker would

    (A) pay social calls to pass the time.

    (B) visit his students' families to find out why they were missing school.

    (C) bring homework assignments to his students in their homes.

    (D) entertain his students and their families with stories about history.

18. Based on the passage, we can infer that the narrator is most likely

    (A) the most dedicated and talented student in class.

    (B) a farmer in an isolated rural community.

    (C) the teacher in a small country school.

    (D) a traveler writing about his trip to a rural community.

19. What reasons do the Eddings give for their children's absence from school?

    (A) The children are being kept home as a punishment.

    (B) The children are needed at home to help with the farm and family.

    (C) The parents don't want their children to become more educated.

    (D) The children don't enjoy school and prefer to stay home.

20. It can be inferred from the passage that Cicero's "pro Archia Poeta" (line 32) is

    (A) a Latin treatise about farming.

    (B) a short story describing the benefits of studying geography.

    (C) a poem about the uneducated.

    (D) not written in simple English.

Go on to the next page ➡

Questions 21–25

1   During the "Golden Age" of Hollywood—
2 from the early 1920s through the early
3 1950s— Hollywood movies were produced
4 and distributed through what is known as the
5 studio system. The term "studio system" refers
6 to two important practices of large motion
7 picture studios at the time: they produced
8 movies primarily on their own filmmaking lots
9 with creative personnel under long-term
10 contracts; and they owned or effectively
11 controlled the movie theaters to which they
12 distributed their films. These two practices
13 helped the top studios maximize their profits
14 and maintain control of the industry.
15   Studios controlled almost completely
16 what jobs the actors under contract with them
17 could or could not do, which was
18 understandably frustrating for some
19 performers. In the late 1930s, Cary Grant
20 became the first Hollywood star to "go
21 independent" by not renewing his studio
22 contract. By leaving the studio system, Grant
23 gained control over every aspect of his career,
24 although he also ran the risk of that career
25 dwindling because no particular studio had a
26 long-term interest in promoting it. For Grant,
27 the risk paid off. Not only was he able to decide
28 which films he was going to appear in, he often
29 had personal choice of his directors and co-
30 stars. At times he even negotiated a share of
31 the gross revenue, something uncommon at the
32 time. Grant received more than $700,000 for
33 his 10% of the gross profits for *To Catch a*
34 *Thief*, while Alfred Hitchcock received less than
35 $50,000 for directing and producing it.
36   Later, the practices that the studio
37 system used to control movie theaters would
38 also come under attack. The studios were
39 investigated by the Federal Trade Commission,
40 which determined that their practices were
41 against the law. At the end of a lawsuit in 1948,
42 they were forced to sell their movie theaters,
43 and give more control over what movies would
44 be purchased and shown to movie theater
45 operators.

Go on to the next page ➡

21. The main purpose of this passage is to

  (A) examine Cary Grant's surprising career choices.

  (B) describe the studio system and its decline.

  (C) demonstrate how larger studios were able to make higher profits.

  (D) argue that long-term contracts are unfair to creative staff.

22. According to the passage, which of the following practices defined the studio system as a method of film production?

  (A) forming long-term contracts with actors and other staff

  (B) paying independent stars like Cary Grant generously for their work

  (C) hiring talented directors like Alfred Hitchcock

  (D) fostering competition among theaters to buy new films

23. The passage suggests that Cary Grant decided to "go independent" (lines 20-21) mainly because

  (A) he wanted to own movie theaters and filmmaking lots.

  (B) he wanted more control over his career.

  (C) he wanted to work with Alfred Hitchcock.

  (D) he wanted to direct and produce his own films.

24. Which of the following questions is answered by information in the passage?

  (A) How much were Grant's co-stars paid for their roles in *To Catch a Thief*?

  (B) Who was responsible for starting the "Golden Age" of Hollywood?

  (C) Were any of the practices of the studio system against the law?

  (D) Who was Cary Grant's favorite director?

25. As it is used in line 31, the word "revenue" most nearly means

  (A) money spent.

  (B) money loaned.

  (C) money lost.

  (D) money earned.

STOP. Do not go on until told to do so.

STOP

SECTION 4

Mathematics Achievement

Each question is followed by four suggested answers. Read each question and then decide which one of the four suggested answers is best.

Find the row of spaces on your answer document that has the same number as the question. In this row, mark the space having the same letter as the answer you have chosen. You may write in your test booklet.

SAMPLE QUESTION: <u>Sample Answer</u>

   Which of the numbers below is NOT a factor of 364?   Ⓐ ● Ⓒ Ⓓ

   (A) 13

   (B) 20

   (C) 26

   (D) 91

The correct answer is 20, so circle B is darkened.

STOP. Do not go on
until told to do so.

MA

1. Which expression is equal to 98?

    (A) $2 \times (9 + 8 + 5)$

    (B) $8 \times (9 + 2) + 5$

    (C) $(8 + 9) + 2 \times 5$

    (D) $8 + 9 \times (2 \times 5)$

2. Jackie has 3 nickels, 4 dimes, and 1 quarter. Jackie puts 40 cents in her piggy bank. How much money does Jackie have left?

    (A) $0.20

    (B) $0.25

    (C) $0.40

    (D) $0.80

3. What is the mean of the following dataset?

    $$2, 3, 5, 6, 7, 7$$

    (A) 4

    (B) 5

    (C) 6

    (D) 7

4. The diagram below shows Terry's collection of black and white marbles.

    If one marble is picked out of Terry's collection at random, what is the probability that it will be a white marble?

    (A) 5 out of 5

    (B) 4 out of 11

    (C) 4 out of 7

    (D) 2 out of 3

5. Alex tracked the weight of a growing kitten, and made a graph. Use Alex's graph to complete the data table.

    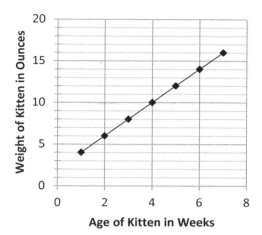

Age	Weight
1 week	4 oz.
2 weeks	6 oz.
5 weeks	a
6 weeks	14 oz.

    What is the value of a in the data table?

    (A) 8 oz.

    (B) 10 oz.

    (C) 12 oz.

    (D) 13 oz.

6. Which expression correctly uses the distributive property to solve $15 \times (8 + 6)$?

    (A) $(15 + 8) + (15 + 6)$

    (B) $(15 \times 8) + 6$

    (C) $(15 \times 8) + (15 \times 6)$

    (D) $(15 \times 8) \times (15 \times 6)$

Go on to the next page ➡

7. How many vertices are there in the cube pictured below?

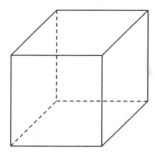

(A) 4

(B) 6

(C) 7

(D) 8

8. Shown below is a floor plan of Ana's bedroom.

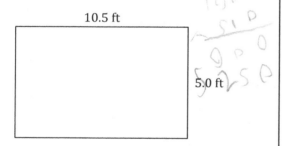

10.5 ft

5.0 ft

Ana is ordering new carpeting for her room so that the entire floor is covered. If her room is 10.5 feet wide and 5.0 feet long, how much carpet will Ana need?

(A) 15.5 ft²

(B) 22.5 ft²

(C) 52.5 ft²

(D) 105.5 ft²

9. Alyssa had a skipping rope that was 15.9 feet long. She cut the rope in half to create two smaller skipping ropes. How long are each of the shorter skipping ropes?

(A) $7\frac{7}{10}$ feet

(B) $7\frac{7}{8}$ feet

(C) $7\frac{19}{20}$ feet

(D) $8\frac{1}{10}$ feet

10. What is the name of the quadrilateral shown below?

(A) Square

(B) Trapezoid

(C) Parallelogram

(D) Rhombus

11. Which number is equivalent to $\frac{3}{4}$?

(A) 0.34

(B) 0.66

(C) 0.75

(D) 3.33

12. A total of 34 students were split into three groups for track and field practice—running, jumping, and throwing. If 12 students were placed in the running group, and 9 students were placed in the jumping group, how many students were placed in the throwing group?

(A) 3

(B) 12

(C) 13

(D) 21

Go on to the next page ➡

13. What is the appropriate equation to determine the height of the triangle in the following diagram ($A = \frac{bh}{2}$ where $A =$ area, $b =$ base, $h =$ height)?

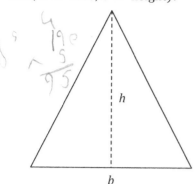

(A) $b = \frac{2A}{h}$

(B) $h = \frac{A}{2b}$

(C) $h = 2Ab$

(D) $h = \frac{2A}{b}$

14. What is the standard form for four hundred fifty thousand two hundred twenty-five?

(A) 425,055

(B) 450,025

(C) 450,225

(D) 452,025

15. Jason buys six bags of candy from the store weighing 47 grams, 112 grams, 695 grams, 619 grams, 98 grams, and 51 grams. What is the estimated total weight of Jason's candy?

(A) between 0 grams and 500 grams

(B) between 500 grams and 1,000 grams

(C) between 1,000 grams and 1,500 grams

(D) between 1,500 grams and 2,000 grams

16. Use the table to answer the question.

STUDENT LUNCH CHOICES					
Lunch	Grade 3	Grade 4	Grade 5	Grade 6	Grade 7
Turkey Sandwich	56	45	40	38	36
Tuna Sandwich	10	11	19	17	15
Salad	7	6	9	13	19

What is the range of this set of data?

(A) 25

(B) 26

(C) 45

(D) 50

Go on to the next page ➡

17. Use the number sequence to answer the question.

1, 4, 10, 22, 46, ___

What is the next number in the sequence?

(A) 68

(B) 70

(C) 87

(D) 94

18. Use the coordinate grid to answer the question. Each grid square has a length of 1 unit.

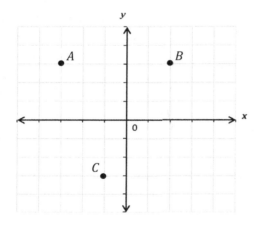

What are the coordinates of point B in the figure?

(A) $(3, 2)$

(B) $(2, 3)$

(C) $(2, -3)$

(D) $(0, 2)$

19. Use the number line to answer the question.

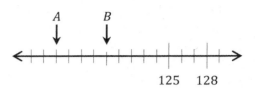

Points A and B represent what numbers?

(A) 107, 115

(B) 115, 119

(C) 116, 120

(D) 140, 135

20. If $\blacklozenge + 9(5 - 3) = 25$, what does $\blacklozenge$ equal?

(A) 47

(B) 43

(C) 41

(D) 7

21. Use the triangle to answer the question.

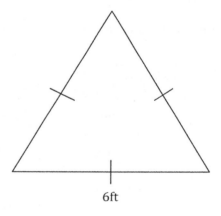

6ft

What is the perimeter of the triangle? $(P = s + s + s)$

(A) 9 ft

(B) 12 ft

(C) 18 ft

(D) 26 ft

Go on to the next page ➡

22. What is the value of the expression 365 + 1,678?

    (A) 1,043
    (B) 1,044
    (C) 2,043
    (D) 2,044

23. Yonge Street is 1,900 kilometers long. Which street has a length closest to 3/4 that of Yonge Street?

    (A) Main Street, which is 1,450km long
    (B) Second Street, which is 1,100km long
    (C) Peter Street, which is 900km long
    (D) Mill Street, which is 425km long

24. The graph shows the number of pizzas given to each class for their pizza parties.

PIZZA GIVEN TO FIVE CLASSES	
Ms. Fredrickson's Class	▽ ▽ ▽
Mr. Johnson's Class	▽ ▽ ▽ ▽ ▽ ▽ ▽ ▽
Mrs. Smith's Class	▽ ▽ ▽ ▽
Mr. Nulman's Class	▽ ▽ ▽ ▽ ▽ ▽
Mr. Kim's Class	▽ ▽

 = 8 slices of pizza

How many more slices of pizza did Mr. Nulman's class get than Ms. Fredrickson's class?

(A) 3
(B) 18
(C) 24
(D) 31

Go on to the next page ➡

25. Which fraction is between $\frac{5}{9}$ and $\frac{19}{27}$?

(A) $\frac{1}{10}$

(B) $\frac{1}{2}$

(C) $\frac{2}{3}$

(D) $\frac{7}{9}$

26. What is the value of the expression 35×42?

(A) 81

(B) 380

(C) 1,280

(D) 1,470

27. The number 11 is

(A) odd and even

(B) odd and prime

(C) even and composite

(D) even and prime

28. Which expression is equal to 75.6×90?

(A) 756×0.9

(B) 756×0.09

(C) 7.56×9

(D) 7.56×900

29. What is the sum of $3.3 + 1.5$?

(A) $4\frac{4}{8}$

(B) $4\frac{7}{10}$

(C) $4\frac{3}{4}$

(D) $4\frac{4}{5}$

30. Four students were asked to walk, jog, and sprint around the track. Their speeds were collected at various times and recorded in the table below.

Times	Walking Student	Jogging Student	Sprinting Student
2 min	5.00 km/hr	11.50 km/hr	20.00 km/hr
4 min	5.00 km/hr	11.00 km/hr	16.00 km/hr
6 min	5.00 km/hr	10.50 km/hr	14.00 km/hr
8 min	5.00 km/hr	10.00 km/hr	13.00 km/hr

At the 6 minute mark, how much faster was the jogging student moving than the walking student?

(A) 9.00 km/hr

(B) 8.00 km/hr

(C) 5.50 km/hr

(D) 5.00 km/hr

STOP. Do not go on until told to do so.

Ivy Global

Essay Topic Sheet

The directions for the Essay portion of the ISEE are printed in the box below. Use the pre-lined pages on pages 36-37 for this part of the Practice Test.

You will have 30 minutes to plan and write an essay on the topic printed on the other side of this page. **Do not write on another topic. An essay on another topic is not acceptable.**

The essay is designed to give you an opportunity to show how well you can write. You should try to express your thoughts clearly. How well you write is much more important than how much you write, but you need to say enough for a reader to understand what you mean.

You will probably want to write more than a short paragraph. You should also be aware that a copy of your essay will be sent to each school that will be receiving your test results. You are to write only in the appropriate section of the answer sheet. Please write or print so that your writing may be read by someone who is not familiar with your handwriting.

You may make notes and plan your essay on the reverse side of the page. Allow enough time to copy the final form onto your answer sheet. You must copy the essay topic onto your answer sheet, on page 36, in the box provided.

Please remember to write only the final draft of the essay on pages 36-37 of your answer sheet and to write it in blue or black pen. Again, you may use cursive writing or you may print. Only pages 36-37 will be sent to the schools.

Directions continue on the next page.

REMINDER: Please write this essay topic on the first few lines of the first page of your essay sheet.

Essay Topic

> **Describe the perfect class field trip. Tell us where your class would go, and what you would do.**

- Only write on this essay question
- Only pages 36 and 37 will be sent to the schools
- Only write in blue or black pen

NOTES

_____
_____
_____
_____
_____
_____
_____
_____
_____
_____
_____
_____
_____
_____
_____
_____
_____
_____

Ivy Global

PRACTICE TEST 2

LOWER LEVEL

HOW TO TAKE THIS PRACTI

To simulate an accurate testing environment, sit at a desk in a quiet location free of di:
computers, phones, music, or noise—and clear your desk of all materials except pe
Remember that no calculators, rulers, protractors, dictionaries, or other aids are allow

Give yourself the following amounts of time for each section:

SECTION	SUBJECT	TIME LIMIT
1	Verbal Reasoning	20 minutes
2	Quantitative Reasoning	35 minutes
5 minute break		
3	Reading Comprehension	25 minutes
4	Mathematics Achievement	30 minutes
5 minute break		
5	Essay	30 minutes

Have an adult help you monitor your time, or use a watch and time yourself. Only give yo
time for each section; put your pencil down when your time is up.

Follow the instructions carefully. As you take your test, bubble your answers into tl
provided. Use the test booklet as scratch paper for notes and calculations. Remember
granted time at the end of a section to transfer your answers to the answer sheet, so yo
you go along.

When you are finished, check your answers against the answer keys provided. Then, s
using the directions at the end of the book.

Ivy Global

1 Ⓐ Ⓑ Ⓒ Ⓓ

2 Ⓐ Ⓑ Ⓒ Ⓓ

3 Ⓐ Ⓑ Ⓒ Ⓒ

4 Ⓐ Ⓑ Ⓒ

5 Ⓐ Ⓑ Ⓒ

6 Ⓐ Ⓑ Ⓒ

7 Ⓐ Ⓑ

8 Ⓒ

9 Ⓒ

10

11

12

13

14

1

2

3

4

5

6

Section 1
Verbal Reasoning

34 Questions	Time: 20 minutes

This section is divided into two parts that contain two different types of questions. As soon as you have completed Part One, answer the questions in Part Two. You may write in your test booklet. For each answer you select, fill in the corresponding circle on your answer document.

PART ONE — SYNONYMS

Each question in Part One consists of a word in capital letters followed by four answer choices. Select the one word that is most nearly the same in meaning as the word in capital letters.

SAMPLE QUESTION:

CHARGE:

(A) release

(B) belittle

(C) accuse

(D) conspire

The correct answer is "accuse," so circle C is darkened.

Sample Answer

Ⓐ Ⓑ ● Ⓓ

Go on to the next page ➡

VR

PART TWO — SENTENCE COMPLETION

Each question in Part Two is made up of a sentence with one blank. Each blank indicates that a word or phrase is missing. The sentence is followed by four answer choices. Select the word or phrase that will best complete the meaning of the sentence as a whole.

SAMPLE QUESTIONS: <u>Sample Answer</u>

    It rained so much that the streets were -------.   ● Ⓑ Ⓒ Ⓓ

    (A) flooded

    (B) arid

    (C) paved

    (D) crowded

The correct answer is "flooded," so circle A is darkened.   Ⓐ Ⓑ Ⓒ ●

    The house was so dirty that it took -------.

    (A) less than ten minutes to wash it.

    (B) four months to demolish it.

    (C) over a week to walk across it.

    (D) two days to clean it.

The correct answer is "two days to clean it," so circle D is darkened.

STOP. Do not go on
until told to do so.

PART ONE – SYNONYMS

Directions: Select the word that is most nearly the same in meaning as the word in capital letters.

1. VOLUNTEER
   (A) aid
   (B) offer
   (C) undergo
   (D) chatter

2. SYNCHRONIZE
   (A) wind
   (B) record
   (C) coordinate
   (D) measure

3. MOURN
   (A) imprison
   (B) lament
   (C) enjoy
   (D) discover

4. GLISTEN
   (A) shorten
   (B) collect
   (C) sparkle
   (D) exhale

5. RELENTLESS
   (A) insistent
   (B) impure
   (C) unfinished
   (D) soft

6. BRAND
   (A) oats
   (B) mark
   (C) business
   (D) bravery

7. RENDITION
   (A) refrain
   (B) article
   (C) song
   (D) version

8. COMMONPLACE
   (A) tasty
   (B) ordinary
   (C) liquid
   (D) invasive

9. HOIST
   (A) drop
   (B) plow
   (C) lift
   (D) strain

10. HEAP
    (A) compost
    (B) roll
    (C) rake
    (D) pile

Go on to the next page ➡

11. SOW

(A) pig

(B) stitch

(C) canal

(D) sour

12. GLEE

(A) gift

(B) depression

(C) joy

(D) clarity

13. LINGER

(A) revert

(B) delay

(C) hurry

(D) remark

14. ADMIRE

(A) impugn

(B) sing

(C) adore

(D) count

15. PERSECUTE

(A) invade

(B) assume

(C) oppress

(D) govern

16. SKEPTICAL

(A) captive

(B) doubtful

(C) tidy

(D) uneasy

17. COUNSEL

(A) letter

(B) monitor

(C) advice

(D) carelessness

Go on to the next page ➡

PART TWO – SENTENCE COMPLETION

Directions: Select the word that best completes the sentence.

18. Harinder was ----------- to learn that his flight was cancelled, as it meant that he would miss his beloved grandfather's birthday party.

    (A) elated

    (B) dismayed

    (C) pleased

    (D) threatened

19. Although they are normally gentle creatures, pigs can become ----------- when forced to live in cramped pens.

    (A) playful

    (B) loving

    (C) aggressive

    (D) fatigued

20. Jake's rabbit was very -----------, and it would not come out of its cage when people were around.

    (A) nautical

    (B) annoying

    (C) political

    (D) timid

21. The beautiful vistas and abundant wildlife of the Galapagos Islands ----------- numerous visitors every year.

    (A) attract

    (B) paint

    (C) repel

    (D) reject

22. Ambreen was ----------- to make a suggestion during the school council meeting, as the school council president did not welcome input.

    (A) hesitant

    (B) excited

    (C) eager

    (D) confident

23. The museum guide told the students they must ----------- from touching any of the exhibits because they can be easily damaged.

    (A) admit

    (B) applaud

    (C) refrain

    (D) retain

24. Eli was the bakery's most ----------- customer; he continued to shop there even though the grocery store had lower prices.

    (A) fickle

    (B) knowledgeable

    (C) neutral

    (D) loyal

25. The story's villain was truly ----------- because he lied to the townsfolk and cheated during his duel with the hero.

    (A) despicable

    (B) relatable

    (C) charming

    (D) forgettable

Go on to the next page ➡

26. Feral cats are notoriously ----------- around people, while their housecat cousins are usually very comfortable with humans.

    (A) bold
    (B) tame
    (C) impervious
    (D) skittish

27. Because dark chocolate is her favorite food, Josie was ----------- to learn that it contains healthy antioxidants.

    (A) ecstatic
    (B) disappointed
    (C) reluctant
    (D) confused

28. Sally was proud of the ----------- in her neighborhood, which was home to people from a variety of countries, religions, and professions.

    (A) repression
    (B) anonymity
    (C) altitude
    (D) diversity

29. Unlike her brother, who never strays far from home, Rebecca -----------.

    (A) does not travel far.
    (B) is a world traveler.
    (C) studies a variety of subjects.
    (D) takes only a small suitcase on her trips.

30. Since Jodhi was a talented chef, -----------.

    (A) she always prepared flavorful dishes.
    (B) her father was an expert baker.
    (C) she respected nature.
    (D) poetry was her favorite thing to read.

31. Although Bret had spent many hours preparing for the test, -----------.

    (A) he performed very well.
    (B) his grade was not as high as he had hoped.
    (C) it covered a wide range of material.
    (D) the entire class had to take it.

32. Logan and his sister enjoyed watching basketball, but -----------.

    (A) often watched games with friends.
    (B) were not talented players themselves.
    (C) followed a number of different teams.
    (D) knew a lot about the sport.

33. I would love to volunteer at the harvest festival, but -----------.

    (A) many students are available to help.
    (B) the festival will involve a variety of activities.
    (C) I believe that volunteering is important.
    (D) I will sadly be out of town that weekend.

34. Although his books have sold millions of copies since his death, F. Scott Fitzgerald -----------.

    (A) was well-known by critics of his era.
    (B) often made money by selling short stories.
    (C) had many financial difficulties during his career.
    (D) made insightful observations about the 1920s in his writing.

STOP. Do not go on until told to do so.

Section 2
Quantitative Reasoning

| 38 Questions | | Time: 35 minutes |

Each question is followed by four suggested answers. Read each question and then decide which one of the four suggested answers is best.

Find the row of spaces on your answer document that has the same number as the question. In this row, mark the space having the same letter as the answer you have chosen. You may write in your test booklet.

SAMPLE QUESTIONS: Sample Answer

What is the value of the expression $(4 + 6) \div 2$?   Ⓐ Ⓑ ● Ⓓ

(A) 2

(B) 4

(C) 5

(D) 7

The correct answer is 5, so circle C is darkened.

A square has an area of 25cm². What is the length of one of its   Ⓐ ● Ⓒ Ⓓ
sides?

(A) 1 cm

(B) 5 cm

(C) 10 cm

(D) 25 cm

The correct answer is 5, so circle B is darkened.

STOP. Do not go on
until told to do so.

1. Which story best fits the equation 24 ÷ 8 = 3?

   (A) Jacqueline gives 8 of her headbands to her friend Lee. How many headbands does she have left?

   (B) Jacqueline has 8 times as many headbands as the number her friend Lee has. If Jacqueline has 24 headbands, how many headbands does Lee have?

   (C) Jacqueline has 8 headbands. If 24 headbands can fit in one bag, how many bags does she need to store her headbands?

   (D) Jacqueline has 24 friends, and each one has 8 headbands. How many headbands do her friends have in total?

2. Use the figure below to answer the question.

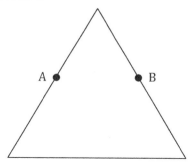

   If the triangle above were cut into two pieces along a straight line between points A and B, the resulting two pieces would be which shapes?

   (A) two rectangles

   (B) a triangle and a square

   (C) a triangle and a trapezoid

   (D) two triangles

3. Use the diagram below to answer the question.

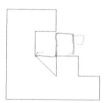

   Which shape completes the square?

   (A)

   (B)

   (C)

   (D)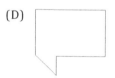

4. Dividing a number N by 6 leaves a remainder of 3. What is the remainder left when $2N$ is divided by 6?

   (A) 12

   (B) 6

   (C) 3

   (D) 0

Go on to the next page ➡

5. Which of the following expressions is equivalent to $0.5 \times ♪ + \frac{★}{2}$?

(A) $2(♪ + ★)$

(B) $0.5(♪ + \frac{★}{2})$

(C) $\frac{♪+★}{0.5}$

(D) $\frac{♪+★}{2}$

6. Use the Venn diagram to answer the question.

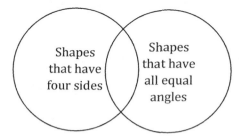

Which shape could be found in the overlapping area of the Venn diagram?

(A)

(B)

(C)

(D)

7. A survey asked 100 students what their favorite season was. The results showed that 50 students prefer summer, 25 students prefer fall, 13 students prefer spring, and 12 students prefer winter. Which of the following circle graphs best represents the data from this survey?

(A)

(B)

(C)

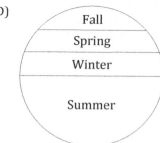

(D)

Go on to the next page ➡

Ivy Global

8. Use the pattern to answer the question.

$$888 = 6 + 9 \times 98$$
$$8{,}888 = 5 + 9 \times 987$$
$$88{,}888 = 4 + 9 \times 9{,}876$$
$$888{,}888 = 3 + 9 \times 98{,}765$$
$$\ldots$$
$$88{,}888{,}888 = 1 + 9 \times m$$

What is the value of *m?*

(A) 9,876

(B) 987,654

(C) 8,888,888

(D) 9,876,543

9. Susan's jar holds 2 cups of water when filled to the top. As shown below, she fills it only partially.

If Susan drinks $\frac{1}{3}$ of the water in the jar and then accidentally spills $\frac{1}{4}$ of the remaining water, how many cups of water are left in the jar?

(A) $\frac{3}{4}$

(B) 1

(C) $1\frac{1}{12}$

(D) $1\frac{1}{4}$

10. Selena is estimating $113.6 \div 11$. Which is the best way for her to estimate?

(A) $100 \div 10$

(B) $100 \div 15$

(C) $113 \div 20$

(D) $150 \div 10$

11. A large cube is built out of smaller cubes, as shown in the diagram below.

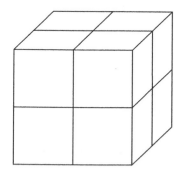

If the volume of the large cube is 32 cubic units, what is the volume of one of the smaller cubes?

(A) 1 cubic unit

(B) 4 cubic units

(C) 8 cubic units

(D) 16 cubic units

12. Which equation can be read as "three times two less than a number is equal to four more than the number"? Let *p* represent the unknown number.

(A) $3 \times (p - 2) = p + 4$

(B) $3 \times (2 - p) = p + 4$

(C) $3 \times 2 \times p = p + 4$

(D) $2 \times (p - 3) = p + 4$

Go on to the next page ➡

13. The graph below shows the medals won by four different countries during the 1988 Summer Olympics.

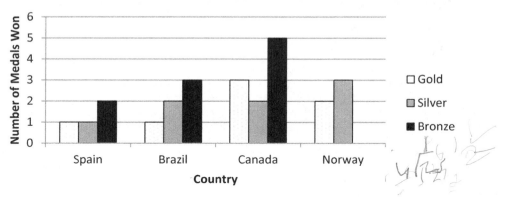

Based on the graph, which conclusion is true about the number of medals won by these four countries?

(A) The median number of silver medals won is greater than the range of bronze medals won.

(B) Brazil's total medal count is less than the number of bronze medals won by Canada.

(C) The median number of total medals won by each country is $5\frac{1}{2}$.

(D) The average (mean) number of gold medals won is greater than the average number of silver medals won.

---

14. It costs $9.95 to buy 1 pound of almonds. Sonja wants to know the price of a bag of almonds weighing 0.48 pounds. Which is the most reasonable estimation for the cost?

(A) $4.00

(B) $5.00

(C) $5.50

(D) $10.50

15. When Samson's two cats both stepped onto a scale, their measured weight was X pounds. When one of the cats got off of the scale, the measured weight was Y pounds. What was the weight of the cat that got off of the scale?

(A) $\frac{Y}{2}$

(B) $X + Y$

(C) $Y - X$

(D) $X - Y$

Go on to the next page ➡

16. If $6 \times m = 42$, which of the number lines shown below shows the correct value of m?

(A)
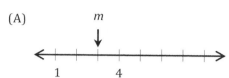

(B)
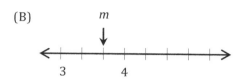

(C)
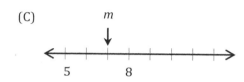

(D)
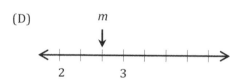

17. Jonathan had a square piece of paper. He cut a square with sides of 1 inch out of the paper, as shown by the dashed lines in the figure below.

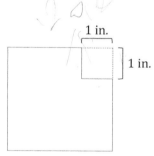

If the perimeter of the original piece of paper was P, what is the perimeter of the paper after it has been cut?

(A) P

(B) $P - 1$

(C) $P + 1$

(D) $\frac{1}{P}$

18. Jaron is plotting a square on a coordinate grid. So far, he has drawn three vertices at the coordinates $(0, 4)$ $(0, -4)$ $(-8, -4)$. To complete the square, what must be the coordinate of the fourth vertex?

(A) $(-8, 0)$

(B) $(-8, 4)$

(C) $(4, -8)$

(D) $(0, 8)$

19. Peter and Amrita both dove off a raft and began swimming in opposite directions. After five minutes, Amrita had swum two hundred meters. If Amrita swims twice as fast as Peter, how far apart were they after five minutes of swimming?

(A) 200 meters

(B) 300 meters

(C) 400 meters

(D) 600 meters

20. The largest square below is divided up into small squares.

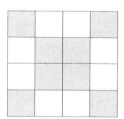

What is the ratio of the shaded region to the unshaded region?

(A) 8:1

(B) 2:1

(C) 1:2

(D) 1:1

Go on to the next page ➡

21. What is the value of R in the math equation $5 - 2R = 1$?

    (A) 2

    (B) 3

    (C) 4

    (D) 5

22. A group of friends is cutting a square card into pieces. The first friend cut it into four equal pieces, and passed it to the second friend. The second friend cut one of those pieces into four equal pieces, and passed it to the next friend, and so on. The figure below shows the card after it has been cut by three people.

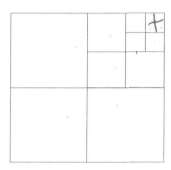

    If the card is cut by one more friend in the same fashion, how many square pieces will there be in total?

    (A) 4

    (B) 9

    (C) 10

    (D) 13

23. Which of the following numbers is greatest?

    (A) 0.309

    (B) $0.\overline{3}$

    (C) 0.334

    (D) 0.099

24. Ayumi has a small model of her bedroom built in her dollhouse. Everything in the dollhouse is built exactly to scale, and her 2-meter-long bed corresponds to a 5-centimeter-long doll bed. If Ayumi's bedroom desk is 1.5 meters wide, how wide is the doll's desk?

    (A) 2.5 centimeters

    (B) 3.75 centimeters

    (C) 4.25 centimeters

    (D) 5.0 centimeters

25. The figure below has three sides with a length of x and three sides with a length of y.

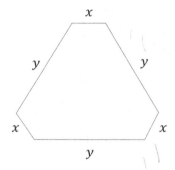

    If $x + y = 11$, what is the perimeter of the figure? (*Perimeter* $= s + s + s + s + s + s$)

    (A) 11

    (B) 14

    (C) 33

    (D) 40

26. Alastair is writing a list of prime numbers less than 50 in ascending order. If the first number on his list is 2, what is the fourth number on his list?

    (A) 5

    (B) 6

    (C) 7

    (D) 11

Go on to the next page ➡

27. Use the table to determine the rule.

Input	Output
✪	✧
1	1.5
3	4.5
8	12
10	15

(A) $✪ + \frac{1}{2}✪ = ✧$

(B) $✪ \times \frac{1}{2} = ✧$

(C) $✪ + \frac{3}{2} = ✧$

(D) $(✪ \times 2) - \frac{1}{2} = ✧$

28. Use the figure below to answer the question.

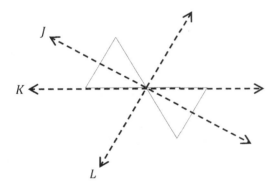

Which line(s) could NOT be a line of symmetry?

(A) J

(B) K

(C) L

(D) J and L

29. Use the equations to answer the question.

$$c - 8 = 1$$
$$3 + d = 5$$

What is the value of $c - d$?

(A) 4

(B) 5

(C) 7

(D) 11

30. Jasmine and her mother have an average of 29.5 spools of thread between the two of them. If Jasmine has 12 spools of thread, how many spools does her mother have?

(A) 29.5

(B) 36

(C) 47

(D) 59

31. The net shown below can be folded into a six-sided cube. Each side has an equal chance of landing face-up when the cube is rolled.

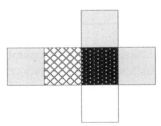

If someone rolls this cube, what is the probability that it will land with a grey side facing up?

(A) $\frac{1}{6}$

(B) $\frac{3}{7}$

(C) $\frac{1}{2}$

(D) $\frac{5}{6}$

Go on to the next page ➡

32. Use the table below to answer the question.

POSTERS COMPLETED BY GROUP MEMBERS	
Group Member	**Number of Posters Completed**
Jessica	2
Augustus	$4\frac{1}{4}$
Lupita	$3\frac{5}{8}$
Hye Su	4
Ciaran	$6\frac{1}{8}$

What was the mean number of posters completed by a single group member?

(A) $3\frac{1}{4}$

(B) 4

(C) $4\frac{3}{8}$

(D) $5\frac{1}{4}$

33. Anton is thinking of a number that is greater than zero but less than six. He then says that it is a composite number. Which could be his number?

(A) 2

(B) 4

(C) 5

(D) 6

34. There are 14 animals in a pet shop which specializes in lizards, birds, and snakes. The total number of legs on these animals is 40, and there are three snakes. If each lizard has four legs and each bird has only two, how many birds are there?

(A) 2

(B) 4

(C) 9

(D) 11

Go on to the next page ➡

35. Linus has twenty-two books that have either gray or black covers. He remembers that he left his bookmark in a book with a gray cover. If he has five books with black covers, what is the probability that his bookmark is in the first gray book he opens?

(A) $\frac{1}{22}$

(B) $\frac{1}{17}$

(C) $\frac{1}{10}$

(D) $\frac{1}{5}$

36. The height and base of a triangle are shown below.

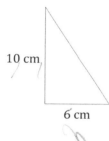

10 cm

6 cm

If the area of a triangle is $A = \frac{1}{2}$ base × height, what is the area of this triangle?

(A) 8 cm²

(B) 16 cm²

(C) 22 cm²

(D) 30 cm²

37. A pond contains goldfish, trout, koi fish, and frogs. If Vikram scoops a net through the pond and randomly catches one animal, he has a $\frac{1}{7}$ chance of catching a frog. Which of the following could be the composition of the pond's animals?

(A) 1 frog, 2 goldfish, 3 trout, 2 koi fish

(B) 1 frog, 8 goldfish, 1 trout, 3 koi fish

(C) 2 frogs, 3 goldfish, 7 trout, 2 koi fish

(D) 7 frogs, 7 goldfish, 7 trout, 7 koi fish

38. Alma has a piece of ribbon that is x feet long. She cuts it into three equal pieces. She then decides that those pieces are too big, and cuts each of the three pieces into five equal pieces. How big is each piece, relative to the total length x?

(A) $\frac{x}{(3 \times 5)}$

(B) $\frac{x}{(3 + 5)}$

(C) $x \times 3 \times 5$

(D) $x - (\frac{1}{3} \times \frac{1}{5})$

STOP. Do not go on until told to do so.

STOP

Section 3
Reading Comprehension

This section contains five short reading passages. Each passage is followed by five questions based on its content. Answer the questions following each passage on the basis of what is <u>stated</u> or <u>implied</u> in that passage. You may write in your test booklet.

Questions 1–5

1   The sun shines with different degrees of
2   heating power at different parts of the world.
3   Where its effect is greatest, such as at the
4   tropics, the air is hottest. Now, imagine that at a
5   certain moment the air all around the globe is
6   at one temperature. Then suddenly the sun
7   shines and heats the air at one point until it is
8   much warmer than the surrounding air. The
9   heated air expands, rises, and spreads out
10   above the cold air. But because warm air has
11   less weight than an equal volume of cold air,
12   the cold air starts to rush towards another
13   point and squeeze the rest of the warm air out.
14   You can picture the atmosphere as made up of
15   a number of colder currents passing along the
16   surface of the earth to replace warm currents

17   rising and spreading over the upper surface of
18   the cold air.
19   Certain air currents interact repeatedly
20   in the same places. For example, temperature
21   differences between mountains and valleys
22   create special air currents called mountain and
23   valley breezes. During the day, air on mountain
24   slopes is heated more than air at the same
25   height over a nearby valley. This warm air rises
26   off the mountain and draws the cool air up
27   from the valley, creating a valley breeze. When
28   the sun goes down, the mountain slopes cool
29   more quickly than the valley air. This cool air
30   sinks, causing a mountain breeze to flow
31   downhill and cool the neighboring valley.

Go on to the next page ➡

1. At line 14, "picture" most nearly means
   (A) imagine.
   (B) paint.
   (C) sketch.
   (D) display.

2. The author's purpose in this passage is to
   (A) confuse.
   (B) entertain.
   (C) educate.
   (D) influence.

3. According to the passage, cold air currents
   (A) rise above hot air currents.
   (B) are created by snow.
   (C) cause storms.
   (D) sink beneath hot air currents.

4. What topic would the author most likely discuss next?
   (A) how air currents affect weather
   (B) qualities of the atmospheres on other planets
   (C) the importance of sunlight for plant growth
   (D) why hot air is less dense than cold air

5. The function of the last paragraph (lines 19–31) is to
   (A) summarize the main idea of the passage.
   (B) provide a specific example of the concept discussed in the first paragraph.
   (C) disprove the concept discussed in the first paragraph.
   (D) leave the reader with a question to consider.

Go on to the next page ➡

Questions 6–10

1   Migration is the regular seasonal
2 movement, often from north to south,
3 undertaken by many species of animals,
4 including birds. Most species migrate due to
5 low levels of food during certain seasons, or in
6 order to breed in a specific place.
7   Migration can be very risky. While on the
8 move, birds are more vulnerable to predators,
9 including human hunters, and can also be
10 harmed by flying into large human structures,
11 such as power lines. People further pose a
12 threat to migratory birds through habitat
13 destruction, which has affected "stopover" sites
14 that birds use for rest during long migratory
15 journeys.
16   While some of the challenges they face
17 may be new, birds have been migrating for
18 thousands of years. Ancient Greek authors
19 recorded the migration of species such as
20 storks, Turtle Doves, and swallows as much as
21 3,000 years ago. More recently, scientists have
22 used new technologies like satellite tracking to
23 observe the migration patterns of a wide range
24 of birds.
25   The distances birds fly to migrate can
26 vary drastically. Some birds that live in
27 mountain ranges, such as the Andes and
28 Himalayas, migrate by simply moving higher
29 up or lower down the mountain depending on
30 the season. By contrast, species such as the
31 Manx Shearwater migrate 14,000 km
32 (8,700 mi) between their northern breeding
33 grounds and the southern ocean. The long-
34 distance migration record for birds belongs to
35 the Arctic Tern, which travels between the
36 Arctic and Antarctic each year.

Go on to the next page ➡

6. This passage is primarily about

    (A) why animals migrate.

    (B) the Manx Shearwater.

    (C) how humans track bird migration.

    (D) bird migration.

7. Which statement about bird migration is supported by information in the passage?

    (A) Bird migration has been observed for at least 3,000 years.

    (B) Migration has become less dangerous for birds in recent years.

    (C) Migration only occurs in mountain ranges like the Andes and Himalayas.

    (D) Birds often become lost during migration.

8. It can be inferred from the passage that the distance flown by the Arctic Tern during migration is

    (A) exactly 14,000 km.

    (B) less than 14,000 km.

    (C) over 14,000 km.

    (D) impossible to calculate.

9. Which question could be answered by information given in the passage?

    (A) How does satellite tracking of birds work?

    (B) What is the best way to track migratory birds?

    (C) What are some reasons birds migrate?

    (D) What are some species of birds that do not migrate?

10. It can be inferred from the second paragraph (lines 7-15) that several of the different threats that birds face during migration are caused in some way by

    (A) habitat destruction.

    (B) new technologies like satellite tracking.

    (C) poor weather.

    (D) people.

Go on to the next page ➡

1   Holi is a spring festival also known as the
2   festival of colors. It is an ancient Hindu
3   religious festival that in recent years has
4   become popular with non-Hindus as well. Holi
5   is primarily observed in India and Nepal, and
6   other regions of the world with significant
7   Hindu, Indian, or Nepalese communities.
8   However, because of its growing popularity,
9   the festival has also spread to parts of Europe
10 and North America.
11   Holi is celebrated at the approach of the
12 spring equinox, on the last full moon day of the
13 month Phalguna, which is the twelfth month of
14 the Hindu calendar. The festival date thus
15 varies every year, but is typically sometime in
16 March or February.
17   The celebrations begin with a bonfire on
18 the night before Holi where people gather, sing

19 and dance. The next morning is a free-for-all
20 carnival of colors. People chase one another
21 with pigmented powder and tinted water,
22 trying to decorate one another with various
23 shades of the rainbow. Some participants get
24 creative with their approach to the festivities,
25 carrying water guns and balloons filled with
26 colored water. Anyone and everyone is fair
27 game: friend or stranger, rich or poor, child or
28 elder.
29   This giant water and color fight occurs in
30 the open streets, public parks, and outside
31 temples and buildings. Groups carry drums and
32 musical instruments, singing and dancing as
33 they move from place to place. People also visit
34 family, friends and even foes, first coloring one
35 another and then staying to laugh, chat, and
36 share Holi delicacies.

Go on to the next page ➡

11. According to the passage, the date of Holi varies because

    (A) its date is based on the full moon and the Hindu calendar.

    (B) people cannot decide when to hold the festival.

    (C) there needs to be good weather so everyone can be outside.

    (D) the festival is growing in popularity.

12. The function of the second paragraph (lines 11– 16) is to

    (A) discuss the importance of Holi.

    (B) describe the festivities that occur during Holi.

    (C) explain when Holi is celebrated.

    (D) argue that Holi should be celebrated during a different month.

13. The mood of Holi celebrations could best be described as

    (A) solemn.

    (B) formal.

    (C) cheerful.

    (D) mournful.

14. Which question could be answered by information given in the passage?

    (A) When was the first Holi festival celebrated?

    (B) What are some favorite Holi delicacies?

    (C) In how many cities is Holi celebrated?

    (D) In what part of a city is Holi celebrated?

15. At line 24, "creative" most nearly means

    (A) productive.

    (B) inventive.

    (C) talented.

    (D) dull.

Go on to the next page ➡

Questions 16–20

1   The Dust Bowl refers to an ecological
2 disaster during the 1930s, when severe dust
3 storms greatly damaged the ecology and
4 agriculture of the U.S. and Canadian prairies.
5 Severe drought and a failure to apply
6 appropriate farming methods to prevent the
7 loss of soil caused the phenomenon.
8   Extensive plowing of the natural
9 topsoil of the Great Plains during the previous
10 decade had displaced the native, deep-rooted
11 grasses that normally trapped soil and
12 moisture, even during periods of drought and
13 high winds. While the area had at one point
14 been considered unsuitable for growing crops,
15 new tools such as gasoline tractors and
16 combine harvesters led to a huge increase in
17 farming, despite the dry climate of the area.
18   These agricultural practices left the area
19 very vulnerable. Because there were no longer
20 grasses to keep the earth in place and retain
21 water, during the drought of the 1930s the
22 loose soil turned to dust. This dust was blown
23 by the strong local wind in large clouds that

24 blackened the sky. These dust storms could
25 become very dangerous, and were called "black
26 blizzards" or "black rollers." On April 14, 1935,
27 20 fierce "black blizzards" occurred all across
28 the Great Plains, from Canada down to Texas.
29 The storms caused extensive damage, and the
30 day became known as "Black Sunday."
31   The drought and erosion of the Dust
32 Bowl affected 100,000,000 acres that centered
33 on the panhandles of Texas and Oklahoma,
34 along with nearby sections of New Mexico,
35 Colorado, and Kansas. This forced tens of
36 thousands of families to abandon their farms.
37 Many of them migrated to California and other
38 states. However, because of the Great
39 Depression, the economic conditions and job
40 opportunities these families found were often
41 just as terrible as those they were trying to
42 escape in the prairies. The plight of such people
43 influenced many famous American artists, such
44 as folk singer Woody Guthrie and novelist John
45 Steinbeck.

Go on to the next page ➡

16. The passage implies that the extensive plowing in the Great Plains, which contributed to the Dust Bowl, took place during

    (A) the 1800s.
    (B) the 1920s.
    (C) the 1930s.
    (D) the 1960s.

17. In line 42 "plight" most nearly means

    (A) pledge.
    (B) predicament.
    (C) success.
    (D) achievement.

18. The primary purpose of the passage is to describe

    (A) the causes and outcomes of the dust bowl.
    (B) the best farming practices for prairie landscapes.
    (C) how people were affected by the great depression.
    (D) how the effects of the dust bowl were reversed.

19. Which word best describes the author's tone?

    (A) critical
    (B) neutral
    (C) admiring
    (D) humorous

20. The function of the last paragraph (lines 31–45) is to

    (A) list popular American artists of the era.
    (B) describe the climate of the American prairies.
    (C) summarize the causes of the dust bowl.
    (D) discuss how people were affected by the dust bowl.

Go on to the next page ➡

1   From a young age, all I wanted to do was
2 write. Dancing was an acceptable pastime, and
3 singing was fine, but neither compared to the
4 thrill of creating stories. It was through writing
5 that I expressed and entertained myself. While
6 my classmates cut up colored paper or
7 experimented with watercolors, I was
8 constructing my next tale. After school, I would
9 routinely reject my neighbor's invitations to
10 play hide-and-seek, preferring to sit inside and
11 compose a new chapter. By writing, I could
12 easily transport myself to other lands, and
13 imagine myself as a fearless warrior or a regal
14 emperor. Best of all, by putting these fantasies
15 on paper, I could revisit them whenever I
16 wanted.

17   My writing process was as follows: first, I
18 would brainstorm a plot. A constant
19 daydreamer, I was rarely short on ideas. Next, I
20 would imagine who could handle the
21 adventures I had planned. My characters were

22 nearly always exaggerated versions of the real
23 people in my life, especially those I looked up
24 to. As soon as these basics were developed I
25 would start to write furiously. Once my pencil
26 touched the page I could not stop, scribbling
27 with the ferocity of a tiny tornado. Finally, I
28 would hand over my draft to my father, who
29 served as my ever-patient transcriber. He
30 would quickly type up my latest masterpiece,
31 handing me each page for my excited review.

32   At the tender age of 9, I undertook to
33 write my first novel. It was a thriller filled with
34 intrigue, mystery, and characters both noble
35 and despicable. Someone had stolen a priceless
36 ruby, and it was up to the story's heroes to
37 track it down. Their quest took them through
38 the capitals of Europe, where they ran up the
39 Eiffel Tower and chased thieves across St.
40 Peter's Square. Though it would be many years
41 before I ever visited these places myself, by
42 writing I felt as if I were already there.

Go on to the next page ➡

21. The passage supports which statement about the narrator?

    (A) Most of her early writing was fiction.

    (B) Her writing simply described the real events in her life.

    (C) She learned to write from her father.

    (D) She was discouraged from writing by those around her.

22. Which best expresses the main idea of the passage?

    (A) The narrator's first novel was published while she was only 9.

    (B) The narrator's constant daydreams seemed like a problem until she began to write.

    (C) The narrator was an enthusiastic writer, even as a child.

    (D) The narrator's first novel spanned the capitals of Europe, from the Eiffel tower to St. Peter's Square.

23. In line 27 "ferocity" most nearly means

    (A) accuracy.

    (B) frenzy.

    (C) fear.

    (D) calm.

24. The passage implies that the author visited Europe

    (A) numerous times as a young child.

    (B) while she was writing her first novel.

    (C) only in her imagination.

    (D) later in her life.

25. The author's attitude toward activities that are not writing is best described as one of

    (A) excitement.

    (B) curiosity.

    (C) sensitivity.

    (D) indifference.

STOP. Do not go on until told to do so.   **STOP**

SECTION 4

Mathematics Achievement

30 Questions

Time: 30 minutes

Each question is followed by four suggested answers. Read each question and then decide which one of the four suggested answers is best.

Find the row of spaces on your answer document that has the same number as the question. In this row, mark the space having the same letter as the answer you have chosen. You may write in your test booklet.

SAMPLE QUESTION:

Which of the numbers below is NOT a factor of 364?

(A) 13
(B) 20
(C) 26
(D) 91

Sample Answer

Ⓐ ● Ⓒ Ⓓ

The correct answer is 20, so circle B is darkened.

STOP. Do not go on
until told to do so.

1. Use the figure below to answer the question.

What is the name of the shape shown in the figure?

(A) kite

(B) rectangle

(C) hexagon

(D) pentagon

2. Jeffrey baked a dozen sugar cookies with different designs on them, as shown in the diagram below.

If his dog randomly eats one of the cookies, what is the chance that it will be a ♥ ?

(A) 1 out of 12

(B) 1 out of 8

(C) 1 out of 6

(D) 2 out of 3

3. The chart below shows the growth of a tomato plant over the course of twelve days.

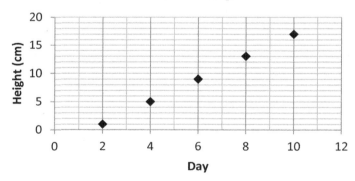

If the plant grew at a constant rate, what was the plant's height on the 7th day?

(A) 17 cm

(B) 11 cm

(C) 7 cm

(D) 6 cm

Go on to the next page ➡

4. Use the triangle to answer the question.

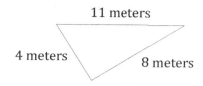

What is the perimeter of the triangle?
($P = s + s + s$)

(A) 12 m

(B) 15 m

(C) 21 m

(D) 23 m

5. Use the number line to answer the question.

What number is represented by point L on the number line?

(A) 18

(B) 22

(C) 25

(D) 29

6. The graph below shows the amount of snowfall in a town over five weeks.

SNOWFALL	
Week 1	❄ ❄
Week 2	❄ ❄ ❄ ❄
Week 3	❄
Week 4	❄ ❄
Week 5	❄ ❄ ❄ ❄ ❄

❄ $= 1\frac{1}{2}$ inches of snow

How much snow fell from the beginning of Week 3 through the end of Week 5?

(A) 3 inches

(B) 8 inches

(C) 12 inches

(D) 14 inches

Go on to the next page ➡

7. A total of 34 people were asked if they preferred cats or dogs. If 17 people said they preferred dogs and 11 people said they preferred cats, how many people did not have a preference at all?

   (A) 28

   (B) 13

   (C) 6

   (D) 0

8. Use the coordinate grid to answer the question.

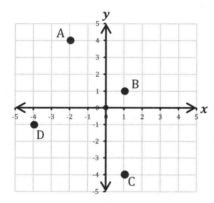

   Which of the four labeled points is closest to the coordinate point (-1, -4)?

   (A) A

   (B) B

   (C) C

   (D) D

9. Use the equations to answer the question

$$3 \times l = 12$$
$$6 + f = 4$$

   What is $\frac{l}{f}$?

   (A) 2

   (B) -2

   (C) 4

   (D) 3

10. A shape is drawn on a coordinate plane.

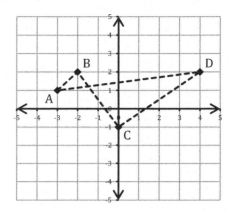

    What are the coordinates of point D?

    (A) (-3, 1)

    (B) (4, 2)

    (C) (-4, 2)

    (D) (-2, 2)

11. Lulu's candy shop charges $1.75 per pound of candy. Nate bought the following amounts of candy:

Candy	Weight
Jellybeans	$\frac{1}{2}$
Sour gummies	$\frac{3}{10}$
Lollipops	$\frac{1}{5}$
Butterscotch	?

    If Nate bought a total of 2 pounds of candy, how much did he spend on butterscotch?

    (A) $1.00

    (B) $1.75

    (C) $2.25

    (D) $3.50

Go on to the next page ➡

12. Which expression is equal to 16?

   (A) $\left(3 - \frac{1}{3}\right) \times 6$

   (B) $3 - \frac{1}{3} \times 6$

   (C) $\left(3 + \frac{1}{3}\right) \times 6$

   (D) $\frac{1}{3}(6 - 3)$

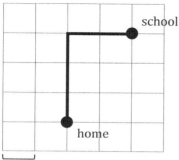

13. The diagram below shows a map of the distance from Solange's school to her house. Each grid on the map represents 2 km.

(grid diagram showing path between school and home)

2 km

If Solange follows the path shown on the grid above, what is the distance that she will walk between school and home?

   (A) 5 km

   (B) 8 km

   (C) 10 km

   (D) 12 km

14. What is the standard form for three hundred fourteen thousand eight hundred twelve?

   (A) 300,412

   (B) 308,142

   (C) 314,812

   (D) 340,812

15. Which list is arranged from smallest to largest?

   (A) $\frac{3}{18}, \frac{3}{6}, \frac{16}{24}, \frac{10}{12}$

   (B) $\frac{3}{6}, \frac{3}{18}, \frac{16}{24}, \frac{10}{12}$

   (C) $\frac{16}{24}, \frac{10}{12}, \frac{3}{18}, \frac{3}{6}$

   (D) $\frac{10}{12}, \frac{16}{24}, \frac{3}{6}, \frac{3}{18}$

16. The transportation department asked a random sampling of people how many times they had taken public transportation in the past month. The results are shown in the stem-and-leaf plot below.

0	2 2 8 8 9
1	2
2	4 6 6
3	0 2 3
4	0 0 0 2 4 6 6 8
5	0 0 2 3 4 4 4 4 4

4 | 6 represents 46 trips using public transportation

How many people took public transportation 30 times or more in the past month?

   (A) 3

   (B) 9

   (C) 20

   (D) 56

Go on to the next page ➡

17. Use the set of numbers shown to answer the question.

{0, 1, 3, 4, 6...}

Which describes this set of numbers?

(A) odd numbers

(B) prime numbers

(C) integers

(D) negative numbers

18. Which expression is equal to 15?

(A) $(7 \times 2) + 5 - 4$

(B) $7 \times (2 + 5) - 4$

(C) $7 \times (2 + 5 - 4)$

(D) $7 \times 2 + (4 - 5)$

19. Pieces from an art collection were sold to different art collectors. Mr. Amati bought $\frac{1}{4}$ of the art pieces, Mrs. Brown bought $\frac{1}{3}$, Ms. Chen bought $\frac{1}{6}$, and Mr. Menounos bought the remainder. If Mr. Amati, Mrs. Brown, and Ms. Chen all donate their portions to a museum, what fraction of the total collection will the museum have?

(A) $\frac{3}{13}$

(B) $\frac{2}{3}$

(C) $\frac{3}{4}$

(D) $\frac{5}{6}$

20. What is the value of the expression 3,200 – 756?

(A) 1,444

(B) 2,444

(C) 2,454

(D) 2,544

21. Use the table to answer the question.

PET OWNERSHIP								
Student	Jason	Priya	Dominic	Nora	Liu	Floyd	Charu	Alex	Leah
Number of Pets	4	0	1	2	2	1	3	6	1

What is the median of this set of data?

(A) 1

(B) 2

(C) 2.4

(D) 4

Go on to the next page ➡

22. What number comes next in the sequence below?

$$1,\ 4,\ 16,\ 64,\ \_\_$$

(A) 60

(B) 68

(C) 256

(D) 264

23. Whitney ran 4 separate times in one week. She completed runs with lengths of 2.25 miles, 3.9 miles, 6.8 miles, and 4. 9 miles. Which is the best estimation for the total number of miles that she ran during the week?

(A) between 17 and 19 miles

(B) between 19 and 21 miles

(C) between 21 and 23 miles

(D) between 23 and 25 miles

24. What is the missing number in the pattern below?

$$1, 1.5, 2, \_\_\_, 3, 3.5$$

(A) 25

(B) 2.5

(C) 2.75

(D) 4

25. Kim's school choir has a total of 83 singers. Which choir has a total number of singers closest to $\frac{1}{4}$ of Kim's choir?

(A) Nasim's choir, with 8 singers

(B) Johan's choir, with 14 singers

(C) Matt's choir, with 17 singers

(D) Husain's choir, with 21 singers

26. If $(3 + \Delta) \times 2 = 14$, what number does Δ stand for?

(A) 2

(B) 4

(C) 7

(D) 9

27. What is the sum of $\frac{1}{3} + \frac{1}{6}$?

(A) 0.11

(B) 0.3

(C) 0.5

(D) 0.6

28. If a rectangle has a length of 3, and an unknown width of w, which equation can be used to determine the rectangle's perimeter? ($P = 2 \times l + 2 \times w$, where P = perimeter, l = length, and w = width.)

(A) $3 \times w$

(B) $3 + w + w + w$

(C) $6 + w$

(D) $6 + 2w$

29. In Marco's science class there are fifteen boy students and twelve girl students. If a student is randomly chosen to go up to the board, what is the chance that the student is a girl?

(A) 1 out of 27

(B) 1 out of 3

(C) 4 out of 9

(D) 5 out of 9

30. The sum of twice a number and five is equal to seventeen. What is the number?

(A) 6

(B) 7

(C) 10

(D) 12

STOP. Do not go on until told to do so.

Essay Topic Sheet

The directions for the Essay portion of the ISEE are printed in the box below. Use the pre-lined pages on pages 78-79 for this part of the Practice Test.

You will have 30 minutes to plan and write an essay on the topic printed on the other side of this page. **Do not write on another topic. An essay on another topic is not acceptable.**

The essay is designed to give you an opportunity to show how well you can write. You should try to express your thoughts clearly. How well you write is much more important than how much you write, but you need to say enough for a reader to understand what you mean.

You will probably want to write more than a short paragraph. You should also be aware that a copy of your essay will be sent to each school that will be receiving your test results. You are to write only in the appropriate section of the answer sheet. Please write or print so that your writing may be read by someone who is not familiar with your handwriting.

You may make notes and plan your essay on the reverse side of the page. Allow enough time to copy the final form onto your answer sheet. You must copy the essay topic onto your answer sheet, on page 78, in the box provided.

Please remember to write only the final draft of the essay on pages 78-79 of your answer sheet and to write it in blue or black pen. Again, you may use cursive writing or you may print. Only pages 78-79 will be sent to the schools.

Directions continue on the next page.

REMINDER: Please write this essay topic on the first few lines of the first page of your essay sheet.

Essay Topic

> **What do you think is the best kind of animal to keep as a pet? Explain why.**

- Only write on this essay question
- Only pages 78 and 79 will be sent to the schools
- Only write in blue or black pen

NOTES

_____

_____

_____

_____

_____

_____

_____

_____

_____

_____

_____

_____

_____

_____

_____

_____

_____

_____

Ivy Global

ANSWER KEYS

CHAPTER 4

PRACTICE TEST 1

LOWER LEVEL

SECTION 1 – VERBAL REASONING (PAGES 40-43)

1. C	6. D	11. A	16. B	21. D	26. B	31. B
2. C	7. B	12. D	17. C	22. B	27. B	32. B
3. D	8. D	13. D	18. C	23. A	28. D	33. C
4. C	9. A	14. A	19. A	24. C	29. C	34. A
5. A	10. D	15. A	20. D	25. A	30. A	

SECTION 2 – QUANTITATIVE REASONING (PAGES 45-52)

1. D	6. B	11. D	16. B	21. A	26. B	31. B	36. C
2. D	7. D	12. A	17. A	22. C	27. C	32. D	37. B
3. B	8. D	13. C	18. B	23. D	28. B	33. A	38. C
4. A	9. A	14. C	19. D	24. C	29. C	34. C	
5. C	10. C	15. B	20. B	25. B	30. B	35. A	

SECTION 3 – READING COMPREHENSION (PAGES 54-63)

1. D	5. A	9. D	13. D	17. B	21. B	25. D
2. B	6. C	10. A	14. D	18. C	22. A	
3. D	7. C	11. C	15. A	19. B	23. B	
4. D	8. A	12. C	16. D	20. D	24. C	

SECTION 4 – MATHEMATICS ACHIEVEMENT (PAGES 65-70)

1. D	5. C	9. C	13. D	17. D	21. C	25. C	29. D
2. C	6. C	10. B	14. C	18. B	22. C	26. D	30. C
3. B	7. D	11. C	15. D	19. C	23. A	27. B	
4. B	8. C	12. C	16. D	20. D	24. C	28. D	

SCORING YOUR TEST

On the ISEE, you receive one point for every question you answered correctly, and you receive no points for questions you answered incorrectly or skipped. In each section, the ISEE also includes 5 or 6 experimental questions that do not count towards your score. You won't be told which questions are unscored, and for this reason, these practice tests do not have specific questions marked as experimental. This also means that it isn't possible to determine an exact score for each section of these practice tests, but you can estimate your score using the procedures below.

To estimate your **raw score** for your practice test, first count up the number of questions you answered correctly in each section. Then, follow the table below to subtract 3, 4, or 5 points for each section, accounting for the experimental questions that would not be scored on your actual ISEE exam.

MY RAW SCORE			
Section	**# of Questions Correct**		**Raw Score**
Verbal Reasoning		– 4 =	28 865–895
Quantitative Reasoning		– 3 =	34 875–905
Reading Comprehension		– 5 =	19 875–905
Mathematics Achievement		– 5 =	25 875–905

SCALED SCORE

Once you have found your raw score, convert it into an approximate **scaled score** using the scoring charts that follow. These charts provide an estimated range for your ISEE scaled score based on your performance on this practice test. Keep in mind that this estimate may differ slightly from your scaled score when you take your actual ISEE exam, depending on the ISEE's specific scaling for that exam and any differences in your own test-taking process.

Ivy Global

Raw Score	Verbal Reasoning	Quantitative Reasoning	Reading Comprehension	Mathematics Achievement
		LOWER LEVEL SCALED SCORE RANGES		
35		875 – 905		
34		875 – 905		
33		870 – 900		
32		865 – 895		
31		865 – 895		
30	875 – 905	860 – 890		
29	870 – 900	860 – 890		
28	865 – 895	855 – 885		
27	865 – 895	850 – 880		
26	860 – 890	850 – 880		
25	855 – 885	845 – 875		875 – 905
24	850 – 880	840 – 870		875 – 905
23	845 – 875	840 – 870		870 – 900
22	845 – 875	835 – 865		860 – 890
21	840 – 870	830 – 860		860 – 890
20	835 – 865	830 – 860	885 – 905	855 – 885
19	830 – 860	825 – 855	875 – 905	850 – 880
18	830 – 860	820 – 850	870 – 900	845 – 875
17	825 – 855	820 – 850	865 – 895	845 – 875
16	820 – 850	815 – 845	860 – 890	840 – 870
15	820 – 850	815 – 845	855 – 885	835 – 865
14	815 – 845	810 – 840	845 – 875	830 – 860
13	810 – 840	805 – 835	840 – 870	830 – 860

12	805 – 835	805 – 835	835 – 865	825 – 855
11	800 – 830	800 – 830	830 – 860	820 – 850
10	800 – 830	800 – 830	825 – 855	820 – 850
9	795 – 825	795 – 825	815 – 845	815 – 845
8	790 – 820	790 – 820	810 – 840	810 – 840
7	785 – 815	790 – 820	805 – 835	805 – 835
6	780 – 810	785 – 815	800 – 830	805 – 835
5	780 – 810	780 – 810	790 – 820	800 – 830
4	775 – 805	780 – 810	785 – 815	795 – 825
3	770 – 800	775 – 805	780 – 810	790 – 820
2	765 – 795	770 – 800	775 – 805	790 – 820
1	765 – 795	770 – 800	770 – 800	785 – 815
0	760 – 790	765 – 795	765 – 795	780 – 810

PERCENTILE

When you take your actual ISEE exam, you will receive a **percentile** ranking comparing your performance against the performance of other students in the same grade who have taken the ISEE that year. For example, a percentile of 62 means that you scored higher than 62% of other ISEE test-takers applying to the same grade. Because your percentile ranking shows how well you performed according to your own grade level, these rankings are frequently given high consideration by admissions offices.

The following charts provide an estimate of your ISEE percentile rankings for this practice test, compared against other students applying to the same grade. For example, if you are scoring at or above the 75th percentile, you are scoring higher than 75% of other ISEE test-takers applying to the same grade. Keep in mind that these percentiles are estimates only, and your actual ISEE percentile will depend on the specific group of students taking the exam in your year.

Ivy Global

LOWER LEVEL VERBAL REASONING PERCENTILES			
Grade Applying To	75th percentile	50th percentile	25th percentile
Grade 5	857	840	821
Grade 6	871	856	837

LOWER LEVEL QUANTITATIVE REASONING PERCENTILES			
Grade Applying To	75th percentile	50th percentile	25th percentile
Grade 5	859	843	828
Grade 6	870	856	840

LOWER LEVEL READING COMPREHENSION PERCENTILES			
Grade Applying To	75th percentile	50th percentile	25th percentile
Grade 5	854	834	815
Grade 6	868	848	828

LOWER LEVEL MATHEMATICS ACHIEVEMENT PERCENTILES			
Grade Applying To	75th percentile	50th percentile	25th percentile
Grade 5	863	848	833
Grade 6	876	863	848

STANINE

When you receive the score report for your actual ISEE exam, your percentile score will also be broken down into a **stanine**. A stanine is a number from 1-9 obtained by dividing the entire range of students' scores into 9 segments, as shown in the table below:

PERCENTILE RANK	STANINE
1 – 3	1
4 – 10	2
11 – 22	3
23 – 39	4
40 – 59	5
60 – 76	6
77 – 88	7
89 – 95	8
96 – 99	9

Although it isn't possible to calculate your exact stanine from this practice test, you can estimate a stanine score range by looking at your estimated percentile score on each section. For example, if you scored between the 50th and 75th percentile in one of your test sections, your stanine score would be between 5 and 6.

Ivy Global

PRACTICE TEST 2

SECTION 1 – VERBAL REASONING (PAGES 82-85)

1. B	6. B	11. A	16. B	21. A	26. D	31. B
2. C	7. D	12. C	17. C	22. A	27. A	32. B
3. B	8. B	13. B	18. B	23. C	28. D	33. D
4. C	9. C	14. C	19. C	24. D	29. B	34. C
5. A	10. D	15. C	20. D	25. A	30. A	

SECTION 2 – QUANTITATIVE REASONING (PAGES 87-95)

1. B	6. B	11. B	16. C	21. A	26. C	31. C	36. D
2. C	7. B	12. A	17. A	22. D	27. A	32. B	37. C
3. A	8. D	13. C	18. B	23. C	28. B	33. B	38. A
4. D	9. A	14. B	19. B	24. B	29. C	34. A	
5. D	10. A	15. D	20. D	25. C	30. C	35. B	

SECTION 3 – READING COMPREHENSION (PAGES 97-106)

1. A	5. B	9. C	13. C	17. B	21. A	25. D
2. C	6. D	10. D	14. D	18. A	22. C	
3. D	7. A	11. A	15. B	19. B	23. B	
4. A	8. C	12. C	16. B	20. D	24. D	

SECTION 4 – MATHEMATICS ACHIEVEMENT (PAGES 108-113)

1. D	5. B	9. B	13. C	17. C	21. B	25. D	29. C
2. C	6. C	10. B	14. C	18. A	22. C	26. B	30. A
3. B	7. C	11. B	15. A	19. C	23. A	27. C	
4. D	8. C	12. A	16. C	20. B	24. B	28. D	

SCORING YOUR TEST

On the ISEE, you receive one point for every question you answered correctly, and you receive no points for questions you answered incorrectly or skipped. In each section, the ISEE also includes 5 or 6 experimental questions that do not count towards your score. You won't be told which questions are unscored, and for this reason, these practice tests do not have specific questions marked as experimental. This also means that it isn't possible to determine an exact score for each section of these practice tests, but you can estimate your score using the procedures below.

To estimate your **raw score** for your practice test, first count up the number of questions you answered correctly in each section. Then, follow the table below to subtract 3, 4, or 5 points for each section, accounting for the experimental questions that would not be scored on your actual ISEE exam.

MY RAW SCORE			
Section	# of Questions Correct		Raw Score
Verbal Reasoning		– 4 =	
Quantitative Reasoning		– 3 =	
Reading Comprehension		– 5 =	
Mathematics Achievement		– 5 =	

SCALED SCORE

Once you have found your raw score, convert it into an approximate **scaled score** using the scoring charts that follow. These charts provide an estimated range for your ISEE scaled score based on your performance on this practice test. Keep in mind that this estimate may differ slightly from your scaled score when you take your actual ISEE exam, depending on the ISEE's specific scaling for that exam and any differences in your own test-taking process.

Ivy Global

LOWER LEVEL SCALED SCORE RANGES				
Raw Score	Verbal Reasoning	Quantitative Reasoning	Reading Comprehension	Mathematics Achievement
35		875 – 905		
34		875 – 905		
33		870 – 900		
32		865 – 895		
31		865 – 895		
30	875 – 905	860 – 890		
29	870 – 900	860 – 890		
28	865 – 895	855 – 885		
27	865 – 895	850 – 880		
26	860 – 890	850 – 880		
25	855 – 885	845 – 875		875 – 905
24	850 – 880	840 – 870		875 – 905
23	845 – 875	840 – 870		870 – 900
22	845 – 875	835 – 865		860 – 890
21	840 – 870	830 – 860		860 – 890
20	835 – 865	830 – 860	885 – 905	855 – 885
19	830 – 860	825 – 855	875 – 905	850 – 880
18	830 – 860	820 – 850	870 – 900	845 – 875
17	825 – 855	820 – 850	865 – 895	845 – 875
16	820 – 850	815 – 845	860 – 890	840 – 870
15	820 – 850	815 – 845	855 – 885	835 – 865
14	815 – 845	810 – 840	845 – 875	830 – 860
13	810 – 840	805 – 835	840 – 870	830 – 860

12	805 – 835	805 – 835	835 – 865	825 – 855
11	800 – 830	800 – 830	830 – 860	820 – 850
10	800 – 830	800 – 830	825 – 855	820 – 850
9	795 – 825	795 – 825	815 – 845	815 – 845
8	790 – 820	790 – 820	810 – 840	810 – 840
7	785 – 815	790 – 820	805 – 835	805 – 835
6	780 – 810	785 – 815	800 – 830	805 – 835
5	780 – 810	780 – 810	790 – 820	800 – 830
4	775 – 805	780 – 810	785 – 815	795 – 825
3	770 – 800	775 – 805	780 – 810	790 – 820
2	765 – 795	770 – 800	775 – 805	790 – 820
1	765 – 795	770 – 800	770 – 800	785 – 815
0	760 – 790	765 – 795	765 – 795	780 – 810

PERCENTILE

When you take your actual ISEE exam, you will receive a **percentile** ranking comparing your performance against the performance of other students in the same grade who have taken the ISEE that year. For example, a percentile of 62 means that you scored higher than 62% of other ISEE test-takers applying to the same grade. Because your percentile ranking shows how well you performed according to your own grade level, these rankings are frequently given high consideration by admissions offices.

The following charts provide an estimate of your ISEE percentile rankings for this practice test, compared against other students applying to the same grade. For example, if you are scoring at or above the 75th percentile, you are scoring higher than 75% of other ISEE test-takers applying to the same grade. Keep in mind that these percentiles are estimates only, and your actual ISEE percentile will depend on the specific group of students taking the exam in your year.

LOWER LEVEL VERBAL REASONING PERCENTILES

Grade Applying To	75th percentile	50th percentile	25th percentile
Grade 5	857	840	821
Grade 6	871	856	837

LOWER LEVEL QUANTITATIVE REASONING PERCENTILES

Grade Applying To	75th percentile	50th percentile	25th percentile
Grade 5	859	843	828
Grade 6	870	856	840

LOWER LEVEL READING COMPREHENSION PERCENTILES

Grade Applying To	75th percentile	50th percentile	25th percentile
Grade 5	854	834	815
Grade 6	868	848	828

LOWER LEVEL MATHEMATICS ACHIEVEMENT PERCENTILES

Grade Applying To	75th percentile	50th percentile	25th percentile
Grade 5	863	848	833
Grade 6	876	863	848

STANINE

When you receive the score report for your actual ISEE exam, your percentile score will also be broken down into a **stanine**. A stanine is a number from 1-9 obtained by dividing the entire range of students' scores into 9 segments, as shown in the table below:

PERCENTILE RANK	STANINE
1 – 3	1
4 – 10	2
11 – 22	3
23 – 39	4
40 – 59	5
60 – 76	6
77 – 88	7
89 – 95	8
96 – 99	9

Although it isn't possible to calculate your exact stanine from this practice test, you can estimate a stanine score range by looking at your estimated percentile score on each section. For example, if you scored between the 50th and 75th percentile in one of your test sections, your stanine score would be between 5 and 6.

Made in the USA
Monee, IL
07 February 2023